The Magic of MENTORING

PEARLS of WISDOM

Barbara A. Perkins, M.A.

Executive Editor: Barbara A. Perkins
Editor: Ava Teherani
Associate Editor: Linda Morgan

Cover Design & Photography: Juan Roberts, Creative Lunacy
Interior Layout: John Sibley, Rock Solid Productions
ISBN: 978-09907199-9-1
Library of Congress Control Number: 2014958934

KNOWLEDGE POWER BOOKS
www.knowledgepowerbooks.com

Printed in the United States

Foreword

Personal experience as both a mentor and mentee brings me to firmly believe that the presence of a caring adult in a young person's life increases self-esteem, strengthens relationships with peers, improves academic performance, and helps prevent school drop-out. Research increasingly indicates that children who succeed, despite enormous personal, economic or social obstacles, do so because of caring competent adults who believe in them.

The magic of mentoring outcomes are reciprocal. Mentors like me attest to enhanced self-esteem, fulfilling expression of personal values, accrued cultural capital, and a 360-degree perspective on the world outside of the circle of privilege.

I believe the mentor/mentee role is a lifelong process. Through each passage of life we evolve and grow. If you are pouring into someone and someone is pouring into you, it provides the lubricant that makes life's machinery and growth process smoother. Where there is less friction, there is more joy. I have committed my life to mentoring, and what a joyous ride it has been.

This is a timely collection of diverse stories. You will be inspired.

George C. Fraser
Author, Speaker, Entrepreneur

Other Books by the Author

Sisters at the Well, Finding and Living Life Lessons
Authority Overrides Power
Seven Little Books on Coaching Yourself Series:
   Coaching Yourself on Marriage
   Coaching Yourself on Grief

The Magic of MENTORING

PEARLS *of* WISDOM

Mark 9:36-37 (KJV)
And he took a child, and set him in the midst of them: and when he had taken him in his arms, he said unto them,
Who so ever shall receive one of such children in my name, receiveth me: and who so ever shall receive me, receiveth not me, but him that sent me.

Dedication

To the wise women who for generations set an intention for me:
Barbara Jane Parrish
Kathleen Louise Marshall
Laurie Lee Gibson
and
Kelsey Nycole Perkins
May all the blessings and love be transferred to you and your
daughters to come.

Special Acknowledgement

In the spirit of Dr. Myles Munroe, a fellow Bahamian, who lived his life as a servant leader and minister of the Gospel of Jesus Christ, I share one of his many quotes.

"The greatest act of a leader is mentoring. Who are you mentoring to take your place? True leaders make themselves unnecessary. A true leader works them-selves out of a job. Study Jesus who was the greatest leader of all times. Listen to His words when he says, *'It is better for me to go away. If I do not go away, you won't be great. My absence is your greatness.'* When Jesus left, His organization grew!"

Dr. Myles Monroe
April 20, 1954 – November 9, 2014

Acknowledgments

Gratitude, appreciation and love are the three words that describe how I feel about Juanita Wright who has been my dearest friend and sister for over 30 years. We began as co-workers at American Airlines in the early 1980's, and 34 years later, we begin most mornings with a telephone call to share the blessings and goodness of God in our lives.

I am grateful for Cheryl Brownlee whose gentle push encouraged me to step out for myself as I have stepped out for others. Your friendship has made a remarkable difference in my life.

I am grateful for Linda Morgan who insisted on my being her big sister, which motivated me to reach higher for us both.

I am grateful for Melrita Fortson, my ride or die partner. Nothing has ever been too much for me to ask of you. Thank you for your love and friendship.

Willa, Alison, Linda, Ava, Maleena, and Juan, you are the amazing team of people I have trusted to help me with this project. It is because of each of you that this book is what it is, a very important tool, intended to change lives for the better. Thank you for caring beyond what was written in your contracts.

To each of the 47 contributors to this book, I pray for God's continual blessings in your life. The collective pearls of wisdom you offered, I know will touch someone in a life-changing way.

Finally, to my friend, spiritual mentor and coach, Dr. Iyanla Vanzant, you taught me how to take a breath, see my whole self, meditate, forgive, listen, release and to tap into my power within. I bow to you as a gesture of the highest respect for who you are.

Close in gratitude,
Barbara Ann Perkins

Contents

Section Three

What Now?

Introduction

All pearls, whether cultivated or natural, share the same properties. An irritant is either implanted in the oyster or by chance a parasite or piece of shell lodges itself inside the oyster and cannot be expelled. However, it happens, nature then creates a magnificent miracle!

A 16-inch necklace requires 47 matching pearls. I read that expert pearl processors cull 10,000 pearls to find 47 that are considered a match. It is a highly specialized skill to find matching pearls. This amazing fact is what I thought about when I invited the 47 contributors to write an essay for this book on mentoring. The 47 contributors to *The Magic of Mentoring: Pearls of Wisdom* are a match in the sense that each of them have demonstrated through their actions and life's work their love and passion for children. They are each mentors themselves and advocates for the importance of having a mentor. They know firsthand about the overwhelming need to find perfect matches for children in cities across this nation in need of all the benefits that positive mentoring will bring to their lives.

There are many types of pearls, but when I think of this group of people whose stories represent the stories of 10,000 others, I think of the Tahitian Pearl, or the Black Pearl as it is most often called. The Tahitian Pearl is a rainbow of colors, which make it a prized possession with additional qualities such as luster, pure surface, clean and without blemishes, great shape and perfect size. These additional qualities are not indicators of the Black Pearl's value alone, but are qualities that cause the Black Pearl to stand out. The men and women sharing their stories in this book stand out, and I am honored to know them and work with them as we collectively advocate and recruit mentors to be matched with our precious children.

The contributors of this book have characteristics I am likening to the Black Pearl, because they are rare individuals who are living their lives in service, and following their heart and passion for helping our most prized possessions, our children. When I am asked to describe what mentoring is to me, I say, "Mentoring is a sincere message from one human being to another that they matter, and that they have a champion for life."

Every child deserves to be mentored. Every child deserves to feel protected and nurtured. Every child deserves to feel that they have a chance at doing and being something great in life. Sadly, this is not our reality. Far too many children will never experience the joy of having someone fully invested in their success. Each morning for six years, after answering the clarion call to action made by our beloved sister, Susan L. Taylor, Founder of the National CARES Mentoring Movement, I asked God for direction and wisdom to contribute something meaningful in my service to others as the leader of the Los Angeles CARES Mentoring Movement.

My life was changed for the better thanks to the never-ending deposits made by the four incredible women who mentored me along the way. Mentoring is low-cost and highly effective. It has been proven through years of research and scores of studies that mentoring works. Therefore, in 2007 when I joined the National CARES Mentoring Movement originally founded as Essence CARES, I was confident that within a few years using the CARES Model of recruiting, all of our children would be rescued. At least that is what I wanted to believe. The unmatched passion of Susan L. Taylor and the rapid growth of the movement was the only indicator I used for that belief. Like the hundreds of dedicated volunteers in cities across America, I was fully in with the National CARES Mentoring Movement and ready to do whatever was necessary to recruit one million mentors to be placed in the lives of the million children waiting and in need of a positive mentoring relationship.

From 2007-2012, I served as the leader of the Los Angeles CARES Mentoring Movement, a circle of local leaders who volunteered to work in tandem with the National CARES Mentoring Movement in developing best practices and strategies for mentor recruitment, and mentor sustainability, once matched with young people. It was a service of love that nourished my soul and provided the opportunity for me to meet some of the most caring and brilliant people in the world. One such person who I have adopted as a younger brother is Stephen Powell, Executive Director of Mentoring USA.

Stephen and I met at a Mentors Retreat in Southern California. It was an instant connection of the hearts. Our trusted bond grew stronger over the years as we spent time in learning and brainstorming sessions. We never hesitated in sharing ideas and opportunities with each other. Although we worked in different organizations, we resisted any notion of competition and always looked for ways to share ideas and resources. Stephen and I talked regularly about the importance of true collaboration and teamwork. We motivated each other when difficulties came up. In many ways, we modeled the mentoring relationships we talked about in our efforts to recruit mentors for young people. Stephen respects and appreciates my formal training in Human and Organizational Development. His firsthand knowledge and experience in the mentoring space far exceeded mine and for me he was the first person I would turn to for help when needed. I appreciate his wisdom, but most of all I appreciate Stephen's unwavering commitment to the children and the absence of ego he demonstrated as a professional.

Cynthia Mitchell Heard, the former Vice President for Program Development at Children Uniting Nations and dedicated member of the Los Angeles CARES Mentoring Movement's board is a force of nature in the mentoring world. She became my sister in the Movement. Her brilliance, success, and notoriety in the mentoring world do not come close to the love and compassion she shows for children in the foster system. Working with Cynthia on developing programs and training workshops for mentors and fundraising events was one of the highlights of my term as local leader for Los Angeles CARES Mentoring Movement.

Her honesty and wisdom guided me. The knowledge she unselfishly shared with me enhanced my confidence to do the work and serve as the first Executive Director for Los Angeles CARES, and the first Executive Director hired by the National CARES Mentoring Movement. It was with Cynthia's help that the Los Angeles CARES circle became one of the model groups in the CARES Movement.

There are many others that I have been blessed to work with and meet through working in the mentoring industry. The entire Los Angeles CARES team, beginning with the original steering committee, to the current board of directors, staff, volunteers, community based partners and founders, each have contributed to my life in such a special way. I will forever be grateful and will continue to be an ambassador and champion for the National CARES Mentoring Movement.

The idea for this book I could contribute to the six years of working as a mentor recruiter. Having to answer the questions hundreds of times, "How do I become a mentor? What is required of me? Do I have what it takes to be a mentor?" I learned quickly that there is no one-way to mentor. I learned that mentors come in all ages and from all backgrounds. I also learned that every story is relatable to someone and that our stories must be told.

The *Magic* *of* MENTORING

PEARLS *of* WISDOM

Section One

Stephen Powell
Executive Director, Mentoring USA
Gratitude for a Myriad of Mentors

My mother, Kirdel Powell, was the first mentor in my life. While having to deal with the untimely loss of her husband, my father, when I was at the tender age of five, she guided me and my brother by instilling the important values of faith, respect, empathy, love, resilience, etc. She, however, was very clear that there would be one critical area of my life where her input would be minimal - facilitating our rites of passage from boyhood to manhood. My mother always encouraged my brother and I to be incredibly discerning with regards to whom we chose as friends. This critical lesson would lead me to two male role models who had a significant impact on my life: my childhood friend, two years my elder, Brian Gibbs, and my high school track and field coach, Richard Kirton.

As a fatherless young man approaching age 14, I found myself in search of guidance from an adult male figure. This crossroad for me was not an uncommon one for most adolescent men. However, it should be noted that this point in time was critical for me in making a decision to seek the influence of a negative mentor or a positive mentor. I chose the latter.

Brian Gibbs invited me to participate in a sport that would help me set goals, build character, exhibit teamwork and build resilience. I would also follow Brian's lead to attend college, thanks to the countless conversations he shared about his experiences as a student at Morehouse. Brian helped make college an attainable reality for me.

My track coach was the father figure who loved me and all of his athletes as if we were his own sons, garnering him the affectionate name "Papa." His workouts were sometimes punishing, but when we were able to see the tangible end result of hard work pay off with victories at a track meet, our weekly contests became great lessons via experiential learning.

The work I do today, as Executive Director at Mentoring USA, is in salute to my late parents and the myriad of mentors who believed in me. As a husband and father of two, I am grateful that God allowed me to meet two individuals I call family.

Susan L. Taylor, Founder of the National CARES Mentoring Movement, I call my mother and earth angel. Barbara A. Perkins, I call sister and coach. These two women are important to me and have proven that mentoring is an important part of their life's work.

Barbara A. Perkins
Author, Life Coach, Mentor
FOUR WOMEN

I am the fifth of ten children. I could say that I might have been the luckiest of the ten. Our dear mother married at sixteen and dropped out of school before completing her high school education. She was only twenty-three years old when I was born and shortly thereafter became a single mother. Needless to say, she needed a lot of help raising five children at that time. She would have five others after me. My mother's, resources and formal education were limited, which made life for her difficult. Our father was in and out of the home and mother could not depend on him with confidence and consistency.

I say that I might have been the luckiest because of **Aunt Kathleen**, my mother's great aunt. She loved her niece so much, that she offered to take her youngest child at the time, which would allow her to go to work without worrying about childcare. That youngest child was me. Aunt Kathleen became my guardian and first mentor from age six to sixteen. She took me to live with her in Nassau, Bahamas, offering to provide whatever I needed without any cost to my mother. Aunt Kathleen made a big commitment and tremendous investment in my life. She loved me and I knew it.

When I reflect on the unmatched gifts of time and resources that Aunt Kathleen gave to me, and how each day she made sure that I knew how special I was, it inspires me to do more and more for others. Aunt Kathleen was my mentor and she expected the best of me always. She gave me wise counsel and was a role model that I continue to emulate. Aunt Kathleen was a woman who had very little materially, but shared generously what she had. In my young mind, she was the Good Samaritan I read about in the Bible. The priceless gifts Aunt Kathleen gave cannot be measured, but those gifts made a positive difference in my life. Without the mentoring of Kathleen Louise Marshall, Barbara Ann Perkins would be someone very different. Every day of my life there is some reminder of a life lesson I received from my beloved Aunt Kathleen, including much of what I would write in this book as core beliefs.

Debra Thompson, my big sister and the most beautiful woman in the world to me, was the second mentor in my life. I do not remember very much about our lives before leaving Miami, Florida, to live in Nassau, Bahamas, with Aunt Kathleen. However, I do remember a few defining events that helped to shape me and each of those events would include my big sister Debra. Debra was my other mother and the person who gave me instructions daily. She was the surrogate mommy in the house. Mother depended on her maturity and brilliance.

When I was about four years old, two critical situations happened to me that I often think about. The first was when I dropped a penny out the bedroom window from the second or third floor apartment we lived in. Determined to retrieve my earned money from the sale of empty soda bottles, I proceeded to go out on the ledge where the penny had landed. My brothers alerted Debra who immediately came to my rescue, a pattern that would repeat itself throughout our lives.

Once I was back in the house safe and sound, my sister lovingly scolded me and assured me that my penny would be replaced. I don't remember if she replaced it or not, but I do recall that I felt comforted and safe as a result of my big sister's intervention. The second memorable occurrence happened months later. We had moved from the apartment in "Over-Town," Miami, and were living in our first house purchased by our maternal grandfather, Sammy McKenzie.

Granddaddy took advantage of the GI Bill that helped veterans purchase their first home. My mother, Barbara Jane, and her sister, Sally Mae, decided to move into this new home with their father, bringing along their six children. My mother had two girls and two boys and Sally Mae had a girl and a boy.

This family setting was great. It was all of our first experience living in a home in a neighborhood with other working-class families. This was a new life for us, and we were all very excited about making new friends and certainly excited about this better life that granddaddy had provided.

Debra made new friends and began to spend time away from the house. She and a group of very beautiful big girls, except none were more beautiful than my sister. They were the local Supremes. They would sew their own dresses and spend time at each other's homes practicing their singing and dancing. I always wanted to go with them, but was repeatedly turned down. One day, I decided that I would follow them to Pat's home. She was the tallest member of the group and had a few brothers that my brothers and I would play with.

On the day that I decided I would follow them, I had just come in from my daily run to the store, "selling bottles." I was entrepreneurial even then. The dress that I had on and wore almost every day had ripped from the waist, and therefore, was longer in the front. My thick jet-black hair needed to be attended to badly. I guess, to Debra I looked a mess! Much later in life, I could see how horrified she must have been as she was developing her relationship with new friends and setting her place in our new neighborhood, to have her little sister, bare-feet and looking a total mess, following her down the street.

When Debra saw me headed her way, she swiftly turned me around. In no uncertain terms I knew she meant business. She told me to go home. That was it, no questions or comments. I cried and ran to the house. As I ran up the stairs of our front porch, I fell and hit my face on the concrete step, opening a cut about an inch on the side of my eye. There was blood everywhere. It was a bad situation. The next thing I remember was being comforted and cleaned up by my big sister. The cleanup included my hair being combed and my clothes being changed. I probably looked as pretty as one of The Supremes.

Debra and I, now fully grown women with children and grandchildren, are best friends. Our lives are connected in so many ways. We love each other as sisters are supposed to. But more than that, Debra and I like each other a lot, and talk almost daily about everything. She is my champion and I am hers. She has been the best role model for any little sister, academically, professionally and in life. Debra is a woman of class and grace. Her beauty runs deep and her personality is equally as beautiful.

Dr. Dorothy Height - When Dr. Dorothy Irene Height died on April 20th, 2010, I immediately began to call around to see where I could help with honoring her legacy and participate in the planning of a memorial service for her in Los Angeles. I wanted to be in Washington D.C., but I knew that there would be so many people in Los Angeles that would not be able to attend the services there, but needed to feel connected to her one last time. I was blessed to be able to do both, and I did.

Fran Jemmott, a well-respected public relations professional in Los Angeles, was one of the women I called first. I knew if we were going to organize a Los Angeles memorial, Fran would be key to the success. She had worked very closely with Dr. Height for years on many projects and was a trusted friend to her. In my conversation with Fran, I wanted her to know that I had been mentored by Dr. Height, and that we shared a very special relationship. After repeating that statement a couple of times, Fran set me straight in the most loving way. She said, "My dear, there is a long line of women who were mentored by Dr. Height." That was one of the reasons she was so admired and adored. Dr. Height made each of the countless women she mentored feel special. When you were with her, you knew those moments were yours and yours alone.

I met Dr. Dorothy in the early 1990's. I moved to Los Angeles in 1985 from New York, married Stanley, and gave birth to Kelsey and Cody. We were living in Sylmar, California, a suburb of Los Angeles. Sylmar was a beautiful community to raise our children. However, it was not as diverse as I would have wanted it to be. We wanted our children to be in a safe neighborhood, with good public schools, but we also wanted them to feel fulfilled and supported culturally.

Stanley introduced me to a group of senior women he had met during the course of his work as a fire inspector. The women were members and local leaders of The National Council of Negro Women (NCNW). These women adopted me soon after our first meeting, and as a result, I was introduced to Dr. Height, the Chair of the Board of Directors for The NCNW. I was literally in awe of Dr. Height. She represented all that was positive and important about black women. I felt blessed to be in her presence, and she sensed it.

While attending my first NCNW convention in New York with another dear sister friend, Gail T. Davis, Mrs. Ester McCall a very close friend of Dr. Height and member of the National Board of NCNW, invited Gail T. and I up to the Presidential Suite. Thank God for Gail T's calm demeanor, because I was so nervous and excited at the same time that I was rendered speechless. We entered the Presidential Suite and walked right into a meeting that Dr. Height was presiding over. She paused from her agenda to welcome and introduce us to the women at the table. We later found out that they were members of the National Board of Directors for NCNW. This was the day my life changed, and I connected with Dr. Height for years to come.

Dr. Height was a mentor who led by example. She did not spend a lot of time telling you how to do something; she simply did it and expected you to be astute enough to understand the significance and the process.

With Dr. Height you learned to be observant and patient. Becoming observant was a lot easier for me than learning to be patient. In fact, patience was slow to come for me. Once I became aware of our goals and the mission, I would want to conquer by way of attack, but Dr. Height was ever so diplomatic and collaborative. She continuously demonstrated the importance of dialogue. Her belief was that if you talked the issue out carefully and heard all opinions, particularly the ones that were different from yours, you would be better prepared to execute. This did not take away from her confidence at all. It was her way of allowing everyone to be a participant. I learned so many lessons from Dr. Height. Rarely does a day go by without me quoting something she would say or repeating a story she may have told. The gigantic spirit of Dr. Dorothy Height fills my private office at home, where a large picture of her hangs over my desk for me to see and draw strength from as I remember our times together.

Ida B. Kinney or Mother Kinney - as she was affectionately called by everyone including local politicians, business people, community leaders, neighbors, family and friends, was my mentor extraordinaire. Linda Jones, Richard Packard, Zedar Broadous, Ken Ashford and others known as community organizers invited me to join them in starting a new chapter of the Black American Political Action Committee (BAPAC). I was relatively new to the Northeast San Fernando Valley, a suburb of Los Angeles. We began working to recruit 50 women to begin a chapter of The National Council of Negro Women. This group came to me with an offer of support for my goal, and a list of questions and recommendations that I later understood was a vetting process for all would-be community organizers. At the top of the list was the question, "Have you met Mother Kinney?"

Whenever Linda Jones and I talk, we often bring up Mother Kinney's name. I have thanked Linda numerous times for that special introduction to Mother Kinney, which began our 17-year friendship. In January 2009, Mother Kinney died at 104 years old, due to complications associated with old age. During the years our friendship grew to be one you could describe as close as a mother and daughter. For a long time I resisted the pull towards each other in that very personal way. Mother Kinney had no biological children. She had grandchildren, nieces and nephews through marriage that she was close to at various stages in their lives, but in her later years, many of those relationships were strained. It made me nervous to be in what I thought was an entangled family situation.

However in 2001, Mother Kinney asked me to become her legal trustee. She gave me power of attorney to her affairs and sought my help with getting her legal matters in order. This took about two years to accomplish and during that time we became even closer. I visited Mother Kinney daily and visited Mr. Kinney, who was in a nursing home nearby, weekly for about five years. She referred to me as her daughter, and to Stanley and my children as her son and grandchildren.

When Mr. Kinney died, she and I planned the services and took care of all of his affairs together. This closeness soon became a relationship that her family targeted negatively, until finally I retreated. In her last two years here, we had not been together very much at all. She was saddened and a bit heartbroken by this and so was I. Thank God we had a chance, before she died, to discuss why we had become disconnected. She apologized to me for listening to what others had convinced her of about me. She acknowledged the untruths, which helped to heal our friendship. I in turn apologized for not being willing to stay the course with her and giving up on our friendship when I could have chosen differently.

The best memories I have of Mother Kinney are how we wrote letters together to politicians. She would have a point of view on an issue, and write notes from her bed. From those notes I would have my speaking points for local commission meetings or interviews with local elected officials who wanted our support or vote. For years at Mother Kinney's request, I would take her completed sample voters ballot from one senior citizen to another. Her sample ballot was the one that others could use to know how to vote. She was an opinion leader on how to vote, and I was a student on how to win friends and influence people politically.

Mother Kinney was 102 when I published my first book, **Sisters at the Well, Finding and Living Life Lessons**. One day she was so excited about my writing that she handed me a check for $1000 and told me that I should use this money towards getting the book completed. She received the first copy of the book for a birthday present. She was so proud of me.

Unfortunately, we did not get to write her book. She wanted to tell her story. Sharing this very short piece about Mother Kinney and the influence she had on my life is, in some ways, fulfilling that dream of her story being told. It is my honor to do so. The legacy of Ida B. Kinney continues, and her spirit lives on through me and hopefully through my children, who will help to keep her memory alive. Maybe one day I will still write her full story.

Now that you have met the four women who have helped to shape me, and who have for as long as I can remember, sowed generously into the well-being of a girl who did not seem to be destined for anything out of the ordinary, you can see how God transforms the ordinary into extraordinary. I find it extraordinary that I've had the experiences that I have had. I find it extraordinary that God would use me in such a small yet significant way as a writer and mentor to others. It is extraordinary to be a living witness to the goodness and truth about who God is, and how he fulfills His promise to each of us. This book and the contributors to this book are all extraordinary people who I am privileged and honored to know.

Brent F. Burton
Fire Captain, Los Angeles County Fire Department
IMMERSED IN MENTORING

I was born and raised in what I considered to be a middle-class section of Los Angeles. My neighborhood consisted primarily of Japanese and African American people. On my block growing up, there were about 20 young men, and all of us had a male role model in our homes. You can't find that today.

According to my family history, I am the youngest of the fifth generation in my family line. Some of my first cousins have children older than me. I always felt as if I were 10 years ahead of my time. In my immediate family, my sister is 13 years older than me, and my brother is 12 years older than me. Many of my cousins are older than me. So I was always drawn to the older people in my family and on my block.

My father was my primary positive male role model. He was a man that got up every morning, shaved, dressed in a suit and tie, drank coffee while he read the morning paper, and then went to work. On the weekends he would handle projects around the house, and when I got out of line, he would handle me.

Because of my father, I became the man that I am today. I could not imagine where or what I would be if it weren't for him in my life. My father was not the only man in my life. There were countless others that encouraged and supported me, and looking back at it now, that was important in my development and growth.

My mother taught me the valuable lessons of being a caring person. Every other month she would take me to the eastside of Los Angeles to visit her elderly aunts and uncles. This gesture taught me how to value your elders. Of course, I could not see or understand it at the time; I understood it as I got older.

I can recall one summer day when school was out, three African American city workers came on our street to trim the trees. I was about 10 years old and I watched them as they scaled the trees and did their job. As they started to clean up the debris, I ran home and got a push broom out of our garage and I started helping them. They took notice of this and encouraged me. At the end of the day, they all pooled their money together and gave me a few dollars for helping. They said they would return tomorrow and I could help them again. I couldn't wait for the next day to come!

When they came back, they gave me a used city yellow hard hat and told me I could wear it when I helped them. This sent me over the moon! I honestly felt like a grown man as I proudly wore my hard hat and helped them clean up. This whole project lasted about 4 days and when they moved onto another street, I sadly waved good-bye and I cherished that opportunity those men gave me to feel needed, wanted and valued! They were mentoring me, but I didn't know it at the time.

Mr. Rolfe was the father of my playmates, Adrian, Annette, Andrea and Angela. He owned a gardening business. During the summer, he would invite me to go to work with him. I jumped at the opportunity to do something productive and what I considered to be fun. Cutting lawns and raking leaves in the summer… fun? That's how I viewed it. Because Mr. Rolfe made work fun!

Mr. Rolfe had customers all over Los Angeles. So off we went. This gave me a chance to see the city and learn about various neighborhoods. He taught me how to use lawn mowers, clippers, blowers, small engines and things like that. As a young man, this was adding to my development. While traveling in his truck, I learned about music as we listened to the radio. Being 4 years younger than his son Adrian, I learned about things a young man should know, as Mr. Rolfe mentored his son and me!

On the block I was drawn to the older kids and what they had to say about being a teenager, and navigating through high school. I learned many lessons listening to my big sis, Stacey Gayle, my big brothers, Dennis Simms, Chuckie, and Darryl Roberts. Kenny Alsup was the father-coach of the block when it came to sports. Growing into my teenage years, I was blessed to be around so many positive and pro-active men and women who helped me grow. Just watching their actions and how they carried themselves modeled the way for me. Joining the Los Angeles Police Department's Explorer program, now called the Cadet program, taught me valuable lessons in leadership and professionalism and gave me a sense of pride to improve myself. LAPD officers, such as officers Matthews and Renty, Artist Gilbert, Bennie Sadler, Eva Jefferson-Welcome, Kim Bragg, Joe Rouzan, Bill Fierro, Godfrey Bascom, Capt. Stan McGarry, Sgt. Ed Payne, Sgt. Ornales, Chief Jesse Brewer and Commander Bernard Parks shaped me into the professional leader I have become today.

As I came closer to pursuing my career goals in the Fire Department, there were countless people there that helped shape me. My cousin, Earl Boyd, the one who introduced me to this profession, spent a lot of time with me. Aquil Basheer, Chauncey Hughes, Millage Peaks, Doug Barry, Don Austin, James Featherstone, Armando Hogan, Mark Viles, Wayne Ibers, Ron Lawrence, Paul Schuster, Floyd Hoffman, Hershel Clady, Anthony Marrone, Ramon Willis, William Mayfield, Michelle Banks, Luther Petty, Joe Tiejera, Isaac Burkes, Dave Burwell, Mark Howell, Andy Kuljis, Eldon Lobdell, Jimmy Hill, Bob LaFever, Kwame Cooper and Carl Holmes were some of the many men and women that helped shape my success in the fire service profession. The pioneers in the fire service who taught me about perseverance were men like Arnett Hartsfield, Wally DeCuir, Grady Bryant, Roger Duncan, Charles Sanders, Robert Ricks, Wince King, Harold Arnold, Bill Lawrence, and Reggie Ballard.

Today, you can say, I am immersed in mentoring. I have personally mentored countless young men and ladies over the span of my career. I currently mentor two young men right now who don't have father figures in their lives.

The stories I have shared and the people I have named have all played an intricate role in my being the man I am today. For those who I did not name for the sake of space, my teachers, coaches, the fathers and mothers of my friends, older cousins, aunts and uncles and my community, I thank you!

I have been blessed to raise three strong children. Being a part of their lives to nurture them stems from my upbringing and how I was mentored.

I thank my parents, my first mentors, for being there as providers and nurturers. I thank Susan Taylor, my adopted big sister, for her vision and making mentoring a call to action. I thank Barbara Perkins, my other adopted big sister, for taping me to run with her as the Los Angeles CARES Mentoring Movement was created.

I once heard a prominent military commander ask this question, "What are the two most important days in your life?" The answer is, the day you're born and the day you realize why you were born. The day I realized why I was born was the day that I realized I was born to mentor others, as I have been mentored throughout my years. It is a shame that more of our African American men don't engage in being mentors. To those brothers that are mentoring, I say thank you and please don't stop! To those brothers that are watching others mentor, I say step up, stand up, get in the game, and help make a difference in a young man's life! We need you!

Sheila Flemming-Hunter, Ph.D.
Founder and President,
The Black Rose Foundation for Children, Inc.

A Calling to Mentor: Love, Acceptance and Caring

The virtues of love, acceptance, and caring are so important when we are in relationship with others, especially with children. When they are combined on behalf of children and deeply rooted in our spirits, the result could be a calling to mentor. It is incumbent upon us to see and think of every child as a gift from God. When our children see and think of adults, they should see and think of us as guides, role models, and mentors. This is my recollection of adults as a child.

I was required to respect adults and recognize their authority. I don't recall ever hearing the word mentor. I heard the words role model more. That's because children were expected to observe more and to say less. Don't get me wrong, I didn't grow up in a world where children were only to be seen and not heard. Rather, I was raised to learn to listen before I spoke and to respect others, especially adults, which often meant being quiet and listening. So, having to look and listen more (or just as much as I would speak), I learned to observe people. As a result, I was able to determine who I could pattern my life after or at least mimic.

My role models were my first mentors, although they would not define themselves that way nor would I. Role models were those whom we admired, sometimes from afar, and wanted to emulate. Mentors were those adults who often took the initiative to be actively involved in a person's life. While I was eventually able to distinguish between the two (role models and mentors), I believe they both had a profound effect on my life. My role models, people I wanted to be like, were both female and male; they ranged from my parents to church members, community leaders and of course my teachers and professors. Later in life I added to my role models people I met at work and those that made contributions in areas I cared about and had an affinity for. For me, role models possess those lofty characteristics that don't change and set the standard for me to follow and/or attain. For example, Mary McLeod Bethune was and is a role model for me (I call her my "Sheroe"), because her life was full of examples of how you can believe in something and then use that faith to motivate you to achieve. She is a model for what I believe is a calling in my life. I wish she could have mentored me.

Thank goodness for the real life role models who can inspire you and in so doing eventually mentor you. That's how I feel about Susan Taylor. She, like Mary McLeod Bethune, has lofty ideals and vision; she inspires me to make a difference, especially in children's lives. I met Susan in Memphis, TN a few years after we established The Black Rose Foundation for Children in Daytona Beach, FL in 2005. With much prayer and investigation about the needs of children in our country and world, we decided to direct the foundation work toward Foster children. We wanted to model the mission of the foundation after the life and work of Dr. Mary McLeod Bethune. Her work was rooted and grounded in the love, acceptance, and care of children. Most of all, we knew she would be involved with children at the deepest level of need.

The vision of our foundation is to ensure that children, especially abandoned children, have unlimited opportunities to excel in all walks of life. The mission is to provide resources to organizations seeking to empower children, through programs, services and advocacy.

But it was meeting Susan and learning about the National CARES Mentoring Movement that I was able to direct the foundation's resources to mentoring children. Mentoring is a cornerstone for programs supported by The Black Rose Foundation for

Children. Where possible, mentoring is included in all we do and support. Our foundation, therefore, became involved in the National CARES business of "securing a generation of children" through mentoring in 2008. We helped establish Memphis CARES Mentoring Movement, and we also partnered with Atlanta CARES Mentoring Movement.

It was also through the National CARES Mentoring Movement that I met Barbara Perkins. Barbara, too, is a role model. She is an example of how our upbringing (learning about who we are and where we came from), and self-love combined with love of God can impact us. We are then empowered to make a difference in others' lives. I am indebted to Barbara for thinking of me when she began to plan this book. Her commitment to children and mentoring are truly magical. The magic, though, is not really mysterious, rather the magic of mentoring is rooted and grounded in love and being open and able to accept and care for children.

For as long as I can remember I have loved children. I cannot think of a time in my life when the presence or sight of children did not make me smile. There is this spirit in me that causes me to see the innocence, the very vision of God, when I see a child. That's why I am always open to mentoring.

In a mentoring relationship with children, adults should know self-love. Openness to mentoring is caused by the desire to share love, understanding that there is vulnerability in mentoring for both mentor and mentee. To be willing to be vulnerable, exhibits the capacity to love unconditionally and to be authentic.

I felt vulnerable when I met one of my mentees who is now supported by our foundation. I met her in Memphis at a community partners' meeting that collaborated around resources and programs for foster children. She, at 20 years old, was the leader of a group of foster children who advocated and educated the community about foster care. At age 16, while in foster care, she had been raped and had a daughter. During the meeting, she told her story about her experience in foster care. Although some of it was sad, she pointed to the good in her life, which included her daughter and her foster parents, whom she now calls her grandparents.

For some reason, perhaps that reason was God (love), I reached out to her and offered to mentor her. She was and still is shy. Her response to my question about mentoring was a timid okay. She did not seem so impressed that this woman, Dr. Sheila Flemming-Hunter, wanted to be in her life. Rather, she seemed to have this wait-and-see attitude. Later, I learned more about foster children, and one of their main challenges is trust. Trust, of course, is key to acceptance and I knew that. I also knew that I had to take the initiative in the mentoring relationship if I was going to gain her trust. So I did. It took some time to get her trust and acceptance, but now, four years later, I know she has accepted me not only as a mentor but also as an example of God's love.

Love is indispensable in a mentoring relationship. Especially a love that is consistent with behaviors that affirm and celebrate a child, who they are and where they are. Acceptance means we are willing to be "present" and to always listen to children. Mentoring in this way helps us bring out the innate essence of children so that they can learn to love themselves, and at the same time have others accept them. Acceptance is an important characteristic of mentoring. You can't fake it; it has to be genuine and authentic. Authenticity sounds complex but indeed it is simple. It means that in the process of being connected to another, especially a child, there is this touching of two spirits recognizing that deep down "I am, because we are."

When a mentor cares, the mentee knows it. Caring opens hearts. Showing that we care gives sight to love. One of my mentors, Dr. Cleo Higgins, always says, "Children don't want to *hear* that you care, they want you to *show* you care." Showing that we care means that we don't have to say everything, do everything or support every decision a child makes. It means there is a knowing that whatever circumstances come their way, the child believes you will be there.

Love, acceptance, and caring can work together to begin, sustain, and grow mentoring relationships that can last a lifetime. I encourage all those reading this essay to take the initiative, whatever your age or status in life, to be a positive force in children's lives. Become a mentor, help recruit mentors, and contribute your time, talents, and treasures to organizations working on children's behalf. Remember, you are a role model who can also be a mentor for children. Most of all, know that mentoring is a calling that if rooted in the spirit of self-love and love for others can transform children's lives.

Maleena Lawrence
Activist and Producer
SEEk WISE COUNCIL

Before I could even begin comprehending the essential necessity and endearing meaning of a mentor, I followed in the shadows of my great grandmother, Emma Johnson. All the grandchildren called her, "MumMum Emma." She was beautiful and rock solid. Definitely she was the cement that held my family together. She did not take no mess and wasn't afraid to tell anyone, "Don't you be bringing no devilish mess up in this house." I didn't know what selfish was because she seemed to always operate in gratitude. Respectfully, MumMum Emma's name and reputation was golden. She taught me so much about God, housekeeping, caring for others, spiritual practices through religion, mending, making use of everything, storing for later, kindness, cooking wild game and baking from scratch.

Before retirement, she was a traveling chef. Never measuring ingredients, MumMum Emma prayed over everything, believed in keeping a strong family and raising a child with good manners. She believed that using manners would take you farther than degrees any day. In other words, "Mind your Manners." This meant at all times respect your elders, use surnames, be sure to say "Thank You", "You're welcome", "Yes", "No", "Please", and many more. These were a part of my basics. Make no mistake, MumMum Emma was very strict about me and my sister Nneka going to church, and staying in school, but she was even more affirming when it came to making sure I "got my lesson."

There were times when we would forget our church clothes on purpose and she would make us wear the same clothes. A classic reminder of "the show must go on." Till this day, I say my prayers;

seek the 'lesson' in everything I do, and the wisdom to know the difference between foolishness and purpose. Wow, as I think about her being one of my first mentors, I flutter like the magic of butterflies beating in my heart. Even now, I laugh out loud because I am still growing and transforming from the roots of her teachings. Spirit knew to pair us early on in my life for reasons I later grew to understand. Seriously, for me to have someone personalize my life out of pure love at a time where my innocence knew not, made me confident and taught me a great deal of independence. The relationship I had with my great grandmother demonstrates the first mentors we come in contact with are family.

Another thing I learned from my MumMum Emma was the spirit of passing it on. Nearly my entire family gave, with no strings attached. Truthfully, this is a pearl that keeps me free from stagnation and allows me to flow in the law of detachment. When I don't, the universe swiftly reminds me to, "Let it go Maleena, if it's meant for you to have, you will." At the end of the day, "Every tub sits on its own bottom", so mind your business and carry on. Yup, and that was what my grandmother Meam would say to me once my MumMum Emma passed away. Jewels never stop dropping; you just have to stay open to catch them. The undeniable beauty that resided in MumMum Emma shined through her daughter, my grandmother Marlene (known as Meam). It was passed on to her daughter, my mother, Carla. Even my father, Donald, still tells me stories of the great Mrs. Emma.

My childhood was preserved like fresh fruit in canning jars. However, the day came where I vividly remember having to adapt and overcome the trials and tribulations of my parents becoming drug addicts. My sister and I went from living in a nice home to a trailer park. Being a teenager at the time, working to carry my household with adult-like responsibilities, was exciting at first and not seen as neglect. Quickly, the obligation of having both parents around but mentally checked out was too heavy. I turned to my godparents, Joanne and Keith White. They were my mediators, mentors and advocates. Although, some conversations came too late to prevent me from experiencing some harsh realities, the balance of my godparents' love, their respect for my parents and understanding, provided me guidance and protection during a time where I could have ended up in a classic statistical situation.

Granted, I was responsible and a strong achiever in school. I knew that my freedom needed structure if I wanted to make it out of my small town in Smyrna, DE, and achieve big dreams of becoming an activist, performer and storyteller. I focused on my goals, learned my lessons, graduated high school working two jobs and got accepted into my favorite HBCU, Norfolk State University. When I went off to college, my aunt Bonnie gave me the best gift in the world, a mustard seed. It sat on a tiny blue cushion in a mini circle gift box. I asked her, "What's this dot, auntie?" She replied, "You know what, it is a nut, it's a seed…" I remember feeling warm and tears lining my eyes when I answered, "Yes, this is a mustard seed huh? The mustard seed of faith." She nodded and told me "Never to lose faith."

Prior to receiving my B.A. degree in Psychology, I minored in Theater, was elected to serve in various leadership roles in Student Government Association and discovered the path of having knowledge of self. My father used to tell me, "Be true to thyself." In college, I got it!

Without looking back, I pre-planned my next move and immediately moved to San Francisco, California. Afterwards, I discovered that the concentration of Black people was in Oakland. During my transition, I healed the relationship between my parents, they got clean and sober and with the help of a phenomenal spiritual teacher named Linda Compton, my life began to soar. She taught me how to swim when I felt like I was alone and drowning.

With a renewed perspective, my life opened up, I met Chauncey Bailey and James Earl "Rocke" Rockerfeller. Chauncey, a respected journalist who wrote for the Oakland Post, taught me what it was to write and convey the truth when sharing community news. Chauncey also wrote my first feature interview. Rocke put me on camera to interview local Indie artists on his entertainment shows that aired on Soul Beat and VJTV. Oakland is where I fell in love with interviewing people and hosting.

Needless to say, I planted my roots in West Oakland and began navigating my new life, new business as a certified massage therapist and production company owner, MaStep Productions with my friend Deborah Stephens. I started hosting and producing The Maleena Lawrence Show, which aired on Comcast public access television station; simultaneously, my mother moved to Oakland and I became an active church member at East Bay Church of Religious Science. It was there where I met two dynamic women, Reverend Elouise Oliver and Reverend Andriette Earl who later founded Heart and Soul Center of Light. They both reflected the wisdom, strength, courage, vision and leadership that attracted and propelled constant growth in my life. I saw a light in Rev. Andriette that called to order my consciousness and she consistently reminded me of the importance of keeping my soul stirred up no matter what life appears to be. Yes, appearances. Rev. Andriette speaks in lyrical metaphors, through her eyes and her smile. Till this day, every now and then she will say, "I see you." Therefore, I feel like she always has a direct sense of where I am in my life.

Years ago, I remember helping Rev. Andriette with a project at church and she told me to come to her house, because she wanted to introduce me to her sister. This was way before I moved to Los Angeles, CA. When I arrived at her home, she introduced me to Mrs. Barbara Perkins. Her hug was warm and she was a beautiful ray of inspirational energy.

When I finally made my move to L.A., Rev. Andriette was being honored and called me to be one of her invited guests at the Sisters At The Well, We See You Awards (WSYA). Much like Mrs. Barbara, who says 'No' to Rev. Andriette? Not I, (chuckles). I was so humbled to be her guest. Just being there with her reassured my move and planted seeds in my spirit that I have work to do - look at all these dynamic women uplifting each other. It made me appreciate the sisters I have in my life as well. Rev. Andriette is the type of mentor that helps me get out of my head, into my heart to do something.

Literally, the world is less than six degrees separation, because when I landed my first full-time job in Los Angeles, I worked for a boutique media company called The Smiley Group. I started off as an event coordinator, touring different cities across the U.S. Eventually, I moved up and became an on-site event producer and rapidly went on to be an associate producer on Tavis Smiley Reports, producing socially conscious content for PBS television programming. Thank God, my background was activism and I previously worked at a lobbying firm before taking on employment in the entertainment industry, because I had to jump in, fly out and learn what to do immediately and strategically.

During my time at TSG, I received both professional mentorship and lifelong friendships. My producer, Sasheen Artis gave me straight production 101 on the job training. Whereas, my friend Eugenia Marshall and then TSG, human resources director, began plugging me into professional circles like Los Angeles African American Women for Public Policy. Guess what? I was reintroduced to Mrs. Barbara Perkins again. In this circle and beyond, Mrs. Barbara taught me about the importance of stepping into leadership, owning my power as a woman, cultivating relationships and balancing life. In order to sustain this level of leadership and impact, I (you too) had to develop and put into practice daily habits that ultimately helped me to identify my own leadership style.

Overall, mentorship has played a leading role in the evolving success of my personal and professional development. When I converse and mentor young girls and women in the various organizations that I support, on the streets or the youth in my family, I desire to speak to their heart. I desire to shift their mindset because I know what it is like to waste time playing on the surface.

Mentorship and a good mentor should inspire you to go deeper in achieving goals, demonstrating your purpose or sharing your skills and talents. When I seek mentorship from my mentors, I ask myself beforehand, what is it that I want and need to learn? Am I willing to do whatever it takes to accomplish the help that I seek? What do I stand to gain from the individual(s) I seek insight from and how will the knowledge or skill set that I obtain help someone else besides me.

Much of my mentorship seems to have been in the form of spiritual teachers, which has helped me stay grounded in everything I do or encounter. Priceless! It is apparent that having and being a mentor is a gift and a required responsibility to be passed on for individuals and communities to thrive.

Penelope Jones-Mensah Mawuenyega, Esq.
Founder of 40 Roses Foundation
Reflections... To Whom Much is Given, Much is Required

Turning 40 was a defining point in my life. It was a point in my life when I would stop and look beyond the ongoing quest for personal satisfaction and embrace the greater fulfillment of depositing lasting treasures into the lives of others. This would force me to reflect on my own journey and the various people on whose shoulders I have stood to become the woman that I am today. These reflections would make crystal clear to me the fact that my individual success is only meaningful when it is used to serve and to advance the greater good.

I was born and grew up in the beautiful West African country of Ghana, to very African parents. Very African in the sense that my father, an outstanding legal luminary who became an Attorney-General of Western Cameroon at the tender age of 28 years, was born to Ghanaian and Sierra-Leonean parents. My mother, a trained teacher, who married him at the tender age of 18 years, was born to Togolese-Ghanaian and Cameroonian parents.

The second girl of the four children in our nuclear family, I was the most assertive and strong-willed. Needless to say, these traits got me into trouble many more times than I want to remember.

Whilst my mother was raising me to be the good African woman that I was expected to be, she would get so frustrated when she would find me deeply engrossed in a book while cooking in the kitchen and totally oblivious to the burning rice on the stove. Being the domestic goddess that she was, she would be mortified. She feared that if I was left to focus solely on my books at the peril of the peculiar socio-cultural expectations of my role as an African woman functioning within the patriarchal society that I was growing up in, I would struggle. And she was right! My mother knew that in order for me to be considered a successful African woman, it would be imperative for me to create a harmonious balance between my career and my domestic role and it was incumbent on her to raise and to mentor me in this direction.

Then there was my high-flyer legal eagle father who expected all of his children, regardless of their gender, to become lawyers just like him. He set the bar for academic achievements very high and the socio-cultural role of the African woman was not to limit me. If Margaret Thatcher could be the Prime Minister of the United Kingdom, so could I, and that's where the discussion ended.

On my journey of self-discovery and personal development, it would become necessary for me to shelve my academic accolades and ambitions, choose my family's special needs, and exercise the right to stay at home to raise our three beautiful children over my legal career for a good ten years. It is during this period that I would appreciate the importance of having mentors in my life who have crashed through glass ceilings to become highly successful leaders of society regardless of the socio-cultural environment in which they found themselves. Some of these incredible African women I found in history, some I found in my own family, and some I found in society.

There was Queen Nana YaaAsantewaa, Queen mother of the Ashanti Kingdom of Ghana, whose life history questions the legitimacy of the perceived role of the indigenous African woman as relegated to the background or to the kitchen as the case may be. In 1900, over a decade before American women were given the right to vote, YaaAsantewaa led the Ashanti people in a war against the British imperial powers of Ghana, after referring to the Asante men as pusillanimous in these famous words:

> *" Is it true that the bravery of Ashanti is no more? I cannot believe it. It cannot be! I must say this: If you, the men of Asante, will not go forward, then we will.*

I shall call upon my fellow women. We will fight till the
last of us falls in the battlefields."

And with this, she took on the mantle of leadership and led the Asante uprising to become a legend in Ghanaian History. She was an African woman. As a mother, a regent and an entrepreneur, she is a role model and a mentor for all women.

My Cameroonian grandmother, Bridget Engome Kanyi-Tometi, taught me silent strength. She was the heart, the spine, and the backbone of our family. She was a true matriarch, but as gentle as a lamb. To her, leadership was always about service to others and she fulfilled her position with integrity. Unquestionably so! She also set the bar very high for me as she mentored me to understand that truth, integrity, and service to others were important qualities for a leader in any sphere of endeavor.

Within and outside of my immediate family, I have been blessed with sterling examples of outstanding women whose life experiences have helped shaped the woman that I am today. An African woman who is not afraid to follow her dreams and to find her own voice and path in a fast, busy world that constantly bombards me with different messages of success- from my culture, my religion, the media, the socio-political institutions, and the rest.

The bold decision to follow my dreams after a ten-year hiatus from my career and to launch straight out from full-time housewife to set up my own law firm and to further extend myself to advocate women's and children's rights, was founded on the need and the courage to be true to myself. I had been empowered to realize my own dreams and to maximize my potential regardless of the glass ceilings I may have encountered in my life. The examples, the accomplishments and the experiences of those before me, facilitated my personal and professional growth and development, formally or informally.

My reflections would highlight for me the importance of encouraging more female leaders in my society and beyond. The need for women to carve out much more space at the top floors of any endeavor, in any country or any culture in the world, notwithstanding the big cultural, historical and biological forces, including the challenge of balancing work and family and other barriers that keep women from being all that they can be. From my reflections, the 40 Roses Foundation would blossom, an initiative that aims at raising women leaders, through education and mentorship, to bring about the needed socio-cultural and economic change and growth in our society.

With women being economic drivers of society and comprising some powerful demographics across the board, any transformational change would depend largely on women taking their seats at the highest decision-making tables and driving some of the initiatives that affect our lives, the lives of our families, our communities, our nations, and the world we live in. Even more important is the responsibility to raise the next generation of women to sit at those tables.

At the 40 Roses Foundation, we harness the power of 40 successful women, to educate, mentor, and empower socio-economically challenged girls, and to enable them to fulfill their God-given potential. We believe that investing in the educational and personal advancement of these girls today means that they will have the tools to re-invest into their own lives, their families and their communities, and they will also become the change agents the world needs.

There are so many girls who need a little help to make it, a little guidance to be able to achieve, a little inspiration to be able to dream bigger, and a little support just to thrive. I am a BIG believer in the power of mentoring and I fully acknowledge that I stand on the shoulders of the strong women like Queen YaaAsantewaa of the Asante Kingdom, My grandma Engome, my mother and the strong women of her day. I also stand on the shoulders of giants like my father who lifts me higher than I could ever fly on my own.

To offer my shoulders to others and to encourage other women to do the same is the least that I can do to ensure that the world that my daughters, Xolasie and Elinam, and my son, Seyram, will inherit tomorrow will be more beautiful than it is today, because we invested

in people, in lives, in dreams, and in causes. I'm still on my journey…
a journey of tremendous opportunities and challenges, a journey of
learning and sharing, a journey of receiving and giving.

I am blessed as I continue to encounter outstanding women
such as Barbara A. Perkins who awed me at our first meeting with her
unflinching commitment to serve humanity. A cause for which she had
travelled all the way from the United States of America with a group
of other dynamic women to Ghana. Their mission was simply, "How
can we help?" Isn't that the true essence of mentoring?

Kimberly Peters
Spoken Word Artist
Mentors Without the Title

Several angels have flown in my life with beauty and courage to enrich and provide hope to my youthful experience. For earthly purposes, I shall call them mentors. With all of the darkness that I was caging myself into due to life planting me in an environment where my parents were not ready to fulfill their duties, I needed a few lifelines. To light my path, initially I was sent one.

Amie L. Peters, my paternal grandmother, was the most valuable teacher. With her strong bowed legs and broad shoulders, she physically represented strength. When one chose not to accept that fact from watching her, they needed to just listen to her shout out in a deep voice, "Yes, Lawd!" She verbalized and modeled all that I was required to know in order to maintain a strong spiritual and physical existence. I do not believe that she was aware of how much strength I would need when she was helping to raise me. I would hide from life under her forearm, and cry in her bosom.

My mother brought me to my grandmother to assist her as a babysitter. Most grandmotherly duties consisted of that. Little did my mother know, I would eventually never want to leave this woman's side. She lifted me up so high that all I could do was fall. I did not know how to fall, but it felt so wonderful when I was flying. My grandmother taught me how to be financially responsible, how to give and receive love, how to stand your ground with conviction, how to make great decisions, and the importance of having a college education.

Mama Amie, as I called her, has been working full-time since she was 15 years old. Growing up in Shreveport, Louisiana, as one of the oldest of thirteen children, provided her the knowledge that independence is invaluable. She always shared her earnings with her family, even after she moved away to Compton, California, the city where I was raised.

Some of the ways my grandmother instilled the importance of independence was by me being able to create opportunities for myself. She kept me involved in the church. She networked so well with the elder members that I received job opportunities, internship opportunities, and scholarship opportunities. She taught me how to listen and be a part of success.

I had loving parents that should've and could've, but didn't. Mama Amie was my divine intervention that I am glad I grabbed a hold of. She was controlling and had an air about her that warranted resistance. Yet, I saw the love and intention, and allowed her to guide me without a sly word in my repertoire… most days. Teenage years are hard on anyone.

I greatly appreciate my grandmother answering the call to be of service. Without her as my lifeline in my childhood and several others in my adulthood, life for me will not have turned out in this manner. Growing into my true self as a gay, Black woman, poet, author and educator, with much judgment and religious manipulation, has been a battle. But, because I knew the Lord for myself, I could not let "nobody turn me around."

Thanks to my grandmother in helping to provide me with a strong foundation. I am a rock that will not crumble when shaken. I am committed to loving myself more than anyone else could ever love me. In her teachings, my grandmother would always say, "They already made it and you gots to make it." I am me, Kimberly Y. Peters, because several people took the time to mentor without the title, but with their love.

April Quiana Russell
Producer/Actress
TEACHING ACCOUNTABILITY,
TRUST AND HONOR

My name is April Quiana Russell; I am a resilient, happy, and extreme deep-thinker. Southern bred from the hills of Chattanooga, TN; I now reside in sunny Los Angeles and wear many hats, including life-long student and mentee.

I enjoy requests like these from Ms. Barbara Perkins, because she challenges me to slow down from my action-packed day and think through how I came to the place I am today, and how has past and present mentorships played a role in my ongoing development.

I was birthed in the principle of valuing and trusting the coaching of mentors and life's teachers. The system of my spiritual, physical and professional life has been shaped through mentorship in my early childhood. I am confident and honored to say, mentorship has chartered my life direction, interrupted tragic pitfalls, and taught me to forgive myself and to forgive. Through mentorship, taking accountability was instilled, as well as visualizing a dream and pushing forward and doing. I was taught to listen to the spirit of God, which is the power inside of me.

This is how April Quiana Russell came to be.

I did not arrive to the place where I am by waking up and simply showing up with a "sound mind" and being the productive and fun soul God has blessed me to become. Ha! I was "Curious George" growing up. I loved life and was never scared to try new things. Unfortunately, my curiosity led me into sticky situations.

The more trouble I got into, the tougher my early mentors were on me. "You reaped consequences for your actions," they told me. As a result I learned accountability. I am a true product of having early childhood courageous epic mentors who impressed upon me the principles of how the blessing of life flows when you take personal responsibility to listen and seek wisdom through mentors. In every lesson, my mentors taught the harsh blunt lessons of the opposite consequences and repercussions of life should I choose not to listen, learn, honor and implement.

I have been blessed to have numerous mentors in various stages of my life. There have been mentors in my life for a season, or for a single event. Then there are tiny special groups who have mentored me since birth.

It is important to understand, mentorship comes in all shapes, sizes and forms. A mentor does not look a certain way, may not have a formal education, and may seem non-mainstream. However, the opportunity to learn and capture the "golden nugget" is priceless. Opening my dictionary APP on my iPad to look up the definition of "mentor," I found a number of adjectives used to describe a mentor: *a wise, trusted, influential counselor, teacher, sponsor or supporter.* The first word that sticks out to me is "trusted." I realize that no matter what area of life or how long a mentor has served in your life, the mentee has a responsibility to trust the mentor and the mentorship given. In order for the relationship to be affective, total trust has to come from the mentee towards the mentor. Without this, the mentorship is of non-effect.

I am noticing and appreciating that the dialogue of the "importance of mentoring" is started to flood our communities and conversations. I love this; however, if there is one message I wish to share, it is to intertwine the message of the "responsibility of the mentee valuing a mentor." We must consciously teach accountability, trust, and honor in the mentor/protégé relationship.

Willa Robinson
Publisher, Knowledge Power Books
Blessed and Highly Mentored

I'm so honored that Mrs. Barbara A. Perkins asked me to write an essay to be included in this phenomenal book, *The Magic of Mentoring: Pearls of Wisdom*. Barbara had been someone I admired for many years by reading the articles she has written and published in the Los Angeles Daily News and Los Angeles Times newspapers. I had always said to myself that one day I would have an opportunity to meet her, and finally, approximately 14 years ago, we met at a funeral in Pacoima, California. Since that time, Barbara has inspired, coached, mentored, encouraged, and allowed me the opportunity to assist her in publishing three of her books. I am blessed to know her.

As the youngest of five, raised by a single mother who worked as a maid for wealthy families living in the suburbs of Kansas City, Missouri, I am a blessed woman. I'm a retired newspaper advertising director, now the publisher of Knowledge Power Books, a company that publishes quality and positive books and educational materials/products that educate, inspire, and motivate children, young adults, and adults to take positive actions and become productive forces in our society. My after-retirement plan was to write and self-publish the Children's Empowerment Book Series, *I Will Be*. Sometimes our best plans don't quite go the way we want them to go; however, I know God had another plan. Now I'm living my BEST life and on purpose.

I am a blessed woman! As I started writing this essay, I thought about all of the powerful people that had a significant impact on me and my life. I realized I was blessed to have a mentor at a very young age, probably 4 or 5 years old. My first mentor was Ms. Charlene Baldwin, a single, beautiful, and extremely creative woman. She was a fashionista in the 50's and 60's. Charlene is a close friend of our family; as a matter of fact, she is family. I have known her all of my life. She spent quality time with me, taking me with her on shopping trip outings with some of her friends. She introduced me as her "play daughter." I was so happy she allowed me in her space. I remember being at her house often. I was privileged to spend time with her and her boyfriend. Charlene was the first woman that I can remember who wore make-up. She arched her eyebrows and wore lipstick.

Charlene made her own high-fashion clothes. During the early years of my life she taught me how to sew. I think I was probably 10 or 11. The first item she helped me make was a pair of yellow "culottes." Yes, culottes. For those of you that don't know what culottes are, they are shorts, short pants that have the look of a skirt. They were a rejuvenated style in the early 60's, later called gauchos. With this skill that Charlene blessed me with, I was able to make clothes, not only for myself, but my sons, my husband, other family members, friends, and at one point in my life, paying customers.

The next mentor in my life was Dr. Inez Kaiser, my home economics teacher at Manual High School in Kansas City, Missouri. At that time, she was Mrs. Kaiser to me. God blessed me with the gift for beautiful penmanship. In elementary school, we practiced penmanship, and I remember writing ovals over and over again. However, my oldest brother and I were blessed with this gift; we really didn't have to practice it. We had the style and art of quality penmanship. One day in class, Mrs. Kaiser noticed my penmanship and asked me if I would like to work for her at her place of business after school. Without thinking about it I said, "Absolutely." She told me that I would be handwriting addresses on invitation envelopes.

We arranged with my mom for Mrs. Kaiser and her husband to pick me up and drop me back home after work. Prior to working for Mrs. Kaiser, I had no idea that she was a public relations professional. At that time, I don't think I even knew what public relations were. I was a freshman in high school. The first day they picked me up to work, I was living on the 10th floor of the Wayne Minor Projects in one of the worse parts of Kansas City. Mrs. Kaiser's office was located in the City National Bank Building in downtown Kansas City, Missouri, on the 10th floor (see the correlation). She may have been the first African American to have an office suite in the building. When I walked into her suite, my eyes nearly popped out of my head. It was the most luxurious office I had ever seen. Actually, it was the only office I had seen, aside from the offices at school. No comparison! Mrs. Kaiser's color scheme was ivory, gold and red, with white/ivory French provincial furniture.

This working experience was my first introduction to the business world. Some days when I was supposed to be addressing envelopes I would dream about being in business one day just like Mrs. Kaiser. This lady mentored me about being a young, black lady in the business world. She mentored me on how to dress in an office environment, how to professionally speak on the telephone, how to write letters and all of the other duties that I could absorb at that particular season in my life. Like any other teenager, regardless of how extravagant I thought the office was, on some days, I just didn't want to work. I wanted to hang out with my friends after school. Mrs. Kaiser had a distinctive way of putting me in my place with her eyes and a strong voice. She would say, "Professional people don't act like that." I believe if it had not been for my experience of working for Dr. Inez Kaiser, my business career would have been quite different or non-existent.

If I could have one more opportunity to sit on the front porch across from my next mentor, Mrs. Lillian Caldwell, aka Crick/Grandma Crickie/Ms. Crick, I would tell her how grateful I am that she took me under her wings and taught me how to be the woman I am today. When Ms. Crick entered my life, I was an immature 16-year old, married and pregnant.

Ms. Crick was my husband's maternal grandmother. She was married to Raymond Caldwell, and they raised five sons and three daughters, as well as her oldest daughter's four youngest children after she passed.

In my opinion, Ms. Crick had all of the qualities of being an excellent mentor:

- A mentor should believe in the mentee.

Ms. Crick believed in me and recognized that I was an intelligent person, although at 16, sometimes I would display certain characteristics that didn't always express my intelligence. She understood that I was a kid and always wanted the best for me.

- A good mentor should be a good listener.

Ms. Crick was an excellent listener and not judgmental. I had the freedom to talk with her about anything, and she listened. One of the BEST things she did for me was to let me know when I was wrong.

- A good mentor should be a role model.

Ms. Crick was a woman of dignity whom everyone in the community respected. She was my role model. As we drank our lemonade on the front porch, I would thank her for believing in me and my husband when no else thought we would make it as a couple. We will reserve the center seat at the head table with her name at our 50th Wedding Anniversary Celebration on February 27, 2015.

Currently, I have been blessed with the wonderful opportunity of helping 23 authors achieve their dreams by publishing their books. In many situations I am a mentor to the authors, and it is my sincere desire to see each one reach their full potential. I not only help them publish their books, but work to inspire, encourage and empower them to be the BEST they can be.

Ebonee Rice
Associate Director, International Black Women Public Policy Institute (IBWPPI)

MENTORING IS PROGRESS

What is progress? How is it measured and how can it be attained? When I think of my personal progress, I am reminded of how much others have contributed to it. My mentors have been an integral part of my personal brand and development. They have simultaneously been my biggest fans and wisest critics.

As a recent college graduate, I have spent the last few years reflecting on how I, a first generation college student, got to this plateau in my life. I realize that it has largely been through the many lunch meetings, phone conversations and silent prayers of my mentors. They have directly impacted my life in such a phenomenal way. Among the things I value most about my relationship with my mentors is the fact that they came organically. I did not seek out a mentor, though I knew I needed one. I believe God divinely and uniquely ordered our steps to cross paths and I am eternally grateful.

For some, mentors come by way of formal acquaintance and inquiry. My path to obtaining a mentor was far less formal. I took a look at the God-loving, beautiful, talented, selfless and motivated women in my life and made sure they did not forget me. I called, emailed, and invited, whatever it took to ensure their continued presence in my life. I like to think that I have likewise made an impact on the lives of my mentors. It is my most earnest prayer that they are proud and pleased with me.

Without the presence of a mentor, I would be traveling through life with no compass. I believe that God has given me mentors to reveal His perfect plan for me, and to encourage me when I feel less than worthy. I also believe that through them I have learned lessons so valuable I would be remise to keep them to myself. Thus, I live my life by the mantra, "Each one, reach one." I make it a point to be a mentor in the lives of young people. What I find is that their experiences often mirrors my own. Their world is often filled with more insecurity, doubt and inadequacy and hope, guidance and wholeness. I get such satisfaction knowing that I can help calm their fears, because my mentors have taught me the power of a touch, a word, and a hug.

I mentor a number of young ladies and men that I know through various organizations. I have watched them mature physically, emotionally, intellectually and creatively. Interestingly enough, my relationship with my mentees has enriched my life immensely. I have learned to be accountable, live with integrity and move through life purposefully. I believe that a mentor is such a special and honorable position to hold in someone's life. As such, mentors have a responsibility to be their best possible self. To accomplish this goal, we must remain true to our moral code of conduct and relinquish what hinders our own personal growth and progression.

In recent years I have learned that there is tremendous need to fulfill humanity's desire for mentors. People are longing for empowerment and inspiration. At some point we all require an extra push to leap into our destinies. One of my life's greatest joys is knowing that I have contributed to a person's freedom from mental prison, guilt, low self-esteem, etc. It is an opportunity responsibility I do not take lightly. If I have provided the same joy for my mentors, I have already lived a successful life. I thank the women who mentored me, for their altruistic attitude, coupled with their desire to reach into my life and leave it better than when they arrived. I will forever live a life of service through mentoring as a way of paying back their zealous love. That, I believe, is how progress is achieved.

Debra Robinson Baker
Executive Director,
Raising Our Youth as Leaders Project
The Influence of Mentoring
is Precious

My name is Debra Robinson Baker. I am a daughter, a spiritual coach, a wife, a writer, and the Executive Director for Raising Our Youth as Leaders Project in Seattle, Washington. I mentor women of all ages and from many walks of life.

I was a petite and dainty child born with cerebral palsy. At the time when most were heading into kindergarten, I was placed in a school with other youth who had been born with physical and mental disabilities. It was in this school that I was introduced to my first mentor. Her name was Bethany, a young girl, but older than me. I spent a good amount of time with her while attending this school. I remember Bethany and her beautiful long braid of red hair well; she taught me so much because she could do nothing for herself. In fact, Bethany required assistance because she was bedridden, and required other people to push her bed from one place to another. In the few months I remained at this school, Bethany invited me to become acquainted with the seed of compassion that was placed in my heart. I did not know then that pushing this beloved girl around and being in this place with these perfectly imperfect individuals would introduce me to the compassion within me. Today I think of Bethany often.

My second mentor that I would identify in life would be my mother. While she has several spiritual and natural daughters, including both my lovely sisters, Jeanette and Leanette Robinson, I am the only daughter she birthed. When I left kindergarten, I was mainstreamed because doctors were certain that I did not have the challenges typically associated with cerebral palsy. From there, my mother took the necessary steps and measures to set up structures and boundaries for me to ensure that I was treated as if I did not have cerebral palsy. We did not deny the disability, she just chose not to give it more space than it required.

It was my mother's concern that others would tease or be unkind to me. Furthermore, she was concerned my grandmother and other relatives might coddle me. For my situation, her decision was a brilliant move. There is a possibility I too would have sabotaged myself, opting out of opportunities by using this challenge as an excuse. Needless to say, I have enjoyed a healthy life, without any indication of cerebral palsy being a part of my life, unless I decide to share it. This taught me to understand the challenges of life but not to allow them to impair my success.

Growing up and yet still a young girl, I would find myself sitting under our family living room table, under the white pressed linen, or perched behind the wall in the hall, eavesdropping on conversations my mother was having with her friends. Most were women of color who came from diverse areas and backgrounds, but who were all a part of the rich fabric of a very young church that we attended in Pasadena, California. These women, too many to name, gave me an introduction to the definition of community. I tasted their recipes and smelled their perfumes. I learned as they responded to life's challenges with a phone call and prayer. I took notice, as their outfits were stylishly fitting and changed in step with the seasons. My mother and these women walked out the definition of what it meant to be a 'Lady,' complete with lace handkerchiefs, slips for their dresses, graceful conversation, and stockings for their beautiful legs.

Moreover, they were unpretentious. They were just young married mothers trying to raise families, sincerely loving God, maintaining themselves, and having great marriages. No doubt they would suggest they were far from perfect. I would argue these young women embodied class, grace, and style. All of these values and attributes I hold close as an adult.

Later, the role(s) my mother played in my life would evolve over and over again. One clear and consistent role that she maintains is that of being my faith coach. I've watched her maintain a marriage for 45 years to the same man. I watch as they are the happiest they've ever been. My mother reminds me that with God ALL things are possible if I seek the Father with my heart.

As I grew and became a young single woman living in the world on my own, I would recognize the treasure I had with having my grandmother and my aunt on my mother's side of the family. I valued the fun holiday traditions the women in our family imparted. Each Thanksgiving and Christmas holiday, my auntie, my grandmother, my mother, and I would call each other days before the holidays and talk food. I started the tradition because I realized I needed their recipes, and one call turned into a conference call or party line, each holiday for several holidays. I learned to make greens, corn bread dressing, Italian cream cakes, Sunday pork roast, and vanilla ice cream by hand, to name just a few recipes. Later, I would stand tall on these recipes as we held large dinner parties at our home, and I gladly did the cooking. With each rave review, I bow in my heart and thank these women in my life.

As I grew, I had many other mentoring experiences that cannot be captured in the traditional sense of mentoring. Rather, most of the additional mentoring I received came in the form of several women and men and the meaningful conversations or "spot mentorship or mentorship moments" I received while in their company. I've sat in the company of great individuals who are celebrities, authors, politicians, deacons, mothers, pastor's wives, judges, lawyers, business owners, executives, artists, and professors. As friends, they invite me into their homes, their spaces, and into their precious experiences. I have learned from them and allowed what I've learned to become pearls of wisdom that assist me today.

One experience of "spot mentorship" happened when I found myself in the company of the magnanimous, Dr. Michael Eric Dyson. He was asked to present the keynote at a fundraiser I attended. It was during this time he became acquainted with my work. What he didn't know was that even though we had been laughing, talking and all seemed well for me, I had been walking through something that was so difficult, it left me in deep pain, exhausted, and wondering if I would make it! In that moment, I was questioning myself when he spoke from his book titled, "Why I Love Black Women." Once he finished, my spirit was repaired, and as I listened to his account of several magnificent women, I watched as he inspired the crowd to places we had not expected. No one wanted to leave that night. Secretly, I was beginning to see myself through a new lens. I was able to catch my breath and finish the hard work of helping those I cared for to heal. I bought his book. I read the stories and began to reorder my direction. As a result, my career advanced greatly. Once again, Dr. Dyson came to town to speak at another event. This time, as a result of his presence, I met the love of my life, Kevin Baker. Needless to say, my life and career have not been the same! Dr. Dyson and his family continue to influence our lives.

I am grateful to all these individuals who have helped to shape my life.

Barbara Perkins and I are sisters. My husband and I were introduced to Barbara a few years ago while at a mutual friend's birthday party. We shared conversation and our hearts connected. Barbara's presence in my life mentors me in ways she is not aware. Barbara is a rare jewel that embodies the spirit of mentorship.

The most important message that I wish to share is that the space of mentoring is precious. The spirit entrusts mentors with a great measure of influence. When managed with grace, this influence the mentor is gifted with, can release dreams, transform lives, nourish broken hearts, and build nations.

Naomi Turner
Administrative Executive
WilliNgNESS, AN ImpORTANT AssET

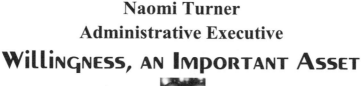

"The greatest good you can do for another is not just to share your riches but to reveal to him his own." - Benjamin Disraeli

I did not have much at the time. I wasn't at the height of my career, didn't have a prince charming, and wasn't driving a luxury vehicle. As a matter of fact, I was only a few years out of college, lived with my sister and my car was over 10 years old. I wasn't "living the life", but still I found myself volunteering to be a mentor to a young girl in Foster care. During the mentor training, in a room full of beautiful, professional, middle-aged women who were looking to give of their time the same way I was, I waited to be asked to leave. I just knew that at any moment the facilitator would ask me to step outside so she could politely suggest I return when I actually had a life worth sharing and some wisdom worth passing down. That moment never came. Somehow they felt me worthy, I made it through. Although to be honest, there was no test, no lie detector to pass and they didn't ask anyone to leave. It was at that moment I realized that my willingness to share me and my time was worth more to this organization than the size of my bank account. Ultimately, this willingness to share my time would prove to be the greatest asset to a successful mentorship.

The organization provided one-on-one mentoring to young girls who were in foster care preparing to transition into adulthood, which meant, much less support from the government including the loss of financial resources and many times homelessness. So I became a one-on-mentor, the scariest kind of the mentoring relationship where success or failure weighed heavy on your efforts. I wasn't as frightened at the prospect as I probably should have been. This naiveté likely came from having been brought up in a large family that included a ton of nieces and nephews, who I shared a great deal of time with. I also grew up with spiritual teachings that instilled in me the desire to volunteer, to think of others and to share what little I had. So through this organization, I was paired with a 15 year-old beautiful girl who was being fostered by her paternal grandmother after her parents, who both suffered from various addictions, were unable to care for her. When we met, she was going to school, working over 30 hours a week since she was required to provide her own food and clothing, and walking long distances to and from these locations in not-so-great neighborhoods. From this I knew she was a survivor and a way-maker.

I would love to say that from the moment we met there was a great connection, but that wasn't the case. There wasn't anything negative or awkward, there just wasn't some magical moment where we looked at each other and felt a tingling. That connection came, but it took some time. I believe this is the case with many mentoring relationships. A lot of the young people, who are a part of these organizations, especially those in foster care situations, have been betrayed by adults much of their lives. It is especially difficult for them to understand why someone who isn't related to them or isn't being compensated to care for them would have any desire to give of their time for nothing in exchange. What I can say of my mentee is that she was open, open to the idea of a mentor, open to sharing her time with me and open to potentially being disappointed by an adult yet again. Her openness was the perfect match for my willingness to share my time.

We began, as all relationships do, with baby steps. There were weekly talks on the phone, dinner, movies, etc. Through the power of consistency and promises met, the barriers melted away. For my role as her mentor, I was conscious of the opportunities to open up her world with dinners at restaurants she had never been to and going to plays and theater performances. Using the moments in the car where I had her as a captive audience to talk about life, sharing my experiences, I asked her about her dreams and goals. It was during these talks that I realized that she, like many young people, had become so used to discouragement by adults, that she belittled her dreams and would talk openly about the goals she knew she could reach with little effort, the ones that required no assistance from anyone else since there were few people she could count on. Of course she didn't state that this was why her dreams were few and easily obtained, I read between the lines. It was my job to hear the whisperings that she sometimes let slip out of the bigger dreams, like college and careers in advertising, of travel and foreign languages. When the whispers came, I made it a point to get excited, talk about details, and let her know that we would find a way to make them happen.

The greatest time of our mentoring relationship came a little over a year after it began. In the beginning of her senior year in high school, her whisperings of bigger dreams had become more powerful and louder. She desired college with her every being. At the beginning of the school year we sat and had a clear, straightforward discussion about our plan to get her to college. She was faced with many obstacles; she was starting a new school where she lost some of her class credits in the transfer, her GPA was a scary 1.8 and even with the classes she planned on taking throughout the year, she would be short two major classes to meet the graduation requirements. In addition, she would still need to work in order to provide some money for herself. After much discussion, a very challenging, but doable plan was laid out for us.

And the year began. For two semesters, her week went as follows: on Mondays, Tuesdays, Thursdays and Fridays, she would walk to school to take her regular classes. Immediately following school, she would attend a 3-hour class to make up one of the courses she needed for graduation. Dinner in hand, I would then pick her up and take her to a different high school to attend a night class for the other course she needed and wait the three hours so that I could take her home. On Wednesdays after school and all day Saturdays and Sundays she would work. She knew that even though the schedule was extremely difficult, she not only had to pass the classes, but she needed to ace at least 11 of the 14 in order to get her GPA college-ready.

She worked so hard that year with little complaints. I realized that she had the drive in her the whole time, she just needed someone to believe in her, hear her dreams, assist her in making a plan, and teach her that when you hear "no" to something you really want, you need to find a new path to your "yes". In the spring of that year, she received an acceptance to San Jose State University and graduated high school with a 3.2 GPA. She has since had a 6-week internship on the other side of the country where she met Oprah, did a semester abroad in London, graduated SJSU and is currently an account manager at a Fortune 500 company. Most of all, she mentors others and shares our story whenever she finds the opportunity.

Charlotte (Char) Bland
Chairperson, Los Angeles CARES Mentoring Movement
THE LIFE LINE TRIBUTE
TO MY AUNTIES

Mentoring is the missing link between a life without hope and a life with vast possibilities. Due to a long-term battle with an illness, my mother was prohibited from caring for her six children as she would have wanted to. Therefore, at nine years old I went to live with aunt Nay, short for Naomi. For about four years under her care and leadership, aunt Nay taught me the basic life skills and how to take care of personal self and basic household fundamentals such as how to wash dishes, mop floors, make beds, cook etc. She was a woman of great discipline, structure and character. Her home was reflective of these characteristics and the pride she had as a homemaker.

Aunt Nay was well respected in the neighborhood and her church community. She was a classy lady who dressed impeccably, always accessorized with a statement-making hat. Under her care, I too was forced to wear a hat every Sunday as part of my church attire. I remember taking it off my head as soon as church was over and clutching it under my arm regardless of how expensive it was (of course I got in trouble not realizing that she was teaching me to be a lady). Throughout my formative years, my family would tease and call me aunt Nay, then and sometimes now, if they want to make a point about how much I am like her. It is true. I have taken on many of aunt Nay's mannerisms and just a bit of her style. You can find me most Sundays at First AME Church, in Los Angeles, sitting in the same section, with my hat and often my gloves on or in my hand always remembering not to talk or chew gum in church.

At 13 years old, I was moved and sent to live with another aunt. Aunt Georgia was a strong black woman who cared for the family and extended family. There were eight people living in her home, 9 including my grandmother who at the time was at the beginning stages of Alzheimer's. All of us depended upon her for everything. It seemed that aunt Georgia worked around the clock, leaving the house at 10 o'clock at night (to work the night shift) and returning in the early morning to begin the work that she did for us at home. All of our basic needs were met and we never went without a meal. To me, aunt Georgia was a warrior woman.

This essay gives me an opportunity to say thank you to the two women who mentored me and who guided me through my journey to adulthood. They both opened their hearts and homes and provided for me in a way that made me feel like I was included. They made me feel that family is important and under no circumstances should we be split up. These are the precious memories that I have to share today as I mentor others. When my grandchildren were at risk of being a part of DCFS, I intervened and told myself, "Aunt Georgia and aunt Nay did it for me, and through their love, it all worked out," so I brought them into my home and mentored them. My life is full of young people, some family and others that I have come to know, who I spend time with as a mentor. It is the giving back that my two special aunts gave me that I think about when I engage with young people.

Five years ago, I met Barbara Perkins, who is one of the founders of Los Angeles African American Women Public Policy Institute, a six month program that prepares women for community leadership and a life of public service. Barbara told the women that service to others was not optional. She would later introduce me to Susan L. Taylor and the National CARES Mentoring Movement. I joined the Los Angeles Circle of Mentors and soon became a member of the board of directors. Today, after five years, I have just taken on the leadership of the Los Angeles CARES Mentoring Movement as the Chair of the board of directors. The mission of the Los Angles CARES Mentoring Movement is to identify, train and match mentors with deserving young people. This term of two years is one that I am excited about and will do my best to make a significant difference in the region.

Tammilee Jules
Poet, Spoken Word Artist
Mentoring that Shaped
and is Guiding My Life

My name is Tammilee Jules. I am a native of Nassau, Bahamas, and the youngest of four siblings. As a child growing up in the Bahamas, I was placed in aftercare with my grandfather, a retired schoolteacher. He had a black board nailed to his Ganip tree in his front yard. There he would have me write and spell words. He would have me play the piano for him to sharpen my skills in all I learned in my music class that day with Mr. Russell, my long time music teacher.

Papa had an organ he played and his example continued to prompt me to study to have him show his approval, which resulted in the reward of earning my practical and theory certificates in music back then. He would sit in his rocking chair in his front yard where he could see all that was happening in the neighborhood. One of the things he continually said to me was "tempus fugit," which means, "time flies." He always told me to be aware of the time and to use time wisely. To this day I am always watching the clock, and I hate anything that blocks me from seeing the time. Having that mindset helps me to be organized and to finish what I start, by putting a start date and deadline on projects and goals.

My aunt, the youngest living girl of my grandfather, was a schoolteacher who was serious about academic excellence. I was placed under her teaching and guidance and she greatly influenced my life. Lori Lee Gibson, my typing teacher, who by her demands for excellence in learning, helped me to achieve my typing certificate and prepare for my BJC's. She was also a very creative arts director. Aunt Lee mentored us into being bold ambassadors for Christ, in speaking publically in church, singing and acting in skits, to share the Gospel before the congregation year after year.

The reason this is so significant is the fact that at my church I am the director of our dance ministry. Like her, I teach the children and the adults of our congregation who have been placed in my care, how to share the Gospel creatively in fine arts and through dance. She is always before me as my living example of following through, being on time and present, ready to work.

My mother, Shirley Boleyn Nixon, taught me by example of how to be a God-fearing wife and mother. She led us to church every Wednesday, Sunday morning and evening. She led our family in devotions every night, and was consistent in her care of our home and her marriage and most importantly her walk with God before us. She took care of everything concerning my father, even though we had a housekeeper. Her word of counsel to me - to always watch the tone of my voice when communicating with my husband - has saved my marriage over these past 21 years.

My mother and father have been married and passionately in love for fifty-four years. They have best friends, my aunt Shirley and Uncle Emil Saunders, who have been with them celebrating the same wedding date for the same number of years. Every year they travel together for their anniversary and have remained best friends without conflict, celebrating their successes and encouraging one another in their failures to move forward. They have seen their children grow together, marry, and now celebrate their grandchildren together.

The significance of their mentorship story has taught me how to form healthy relationships. They have shown me that it is possible to have lifelong, authentic, joyful friendships without conflict, backbiting, competitiveness, and jealousy or confusion.

My late - but far from forgotten mentor - Pastor Kitt Brewington, taught me how to be a strong woman of faith. She taught me how to study the Word of God, and know it for myself, with full understanding of its truth. She taught me how to be led by the Holy Spirit in all things, and how to be true to myself, and a true worshiper before God. She taught me by her life how to fight the good fight of faith and take courage in doing so. Her last words to us, "Discouragement is a choice, take courage!" This has caused me to continue to rise above adversity and keep it moving forward.

Last but definitely not least, my mentor to this day is Barbara Perkins. I have learned from Barbara how to take the grand vision God has given me and soar with it with determination, perseverance, and fearlessness in excellence across the board. Barbara teaches me how to kick the barriers down and keep it moving on track to reaching my goals. My father always said to us growing up, "A job worth doing is worth doing well... it's your signature." I have seen the importance of a good name through Barbara's continued climb to levels and realms bigger than her, and the respect she has gained from her reputation of producing the best quality work or events she has been assigned to and entrusted with. She has taught me how to take a leap of faith through open doors of opportunity, and then present myself well once I am given the microphone.

I have learned how to stand before giants and fight back without fear but in faith and watch God handle it (He prepares a table before me in the presence of my enemies). Barbara's life story has helped me get up from places that caused me pain to press forward like her. She has taught me how to embrace life and be comfortable sharing even the deepest wounds when its purpose is to help others.

Her mentorship has taught me how to have a voice for the oppressed and how to use it effectively to sound the alarm when something is wrong, and that we need all hands-on deck to make it right. She has taught me how to be comfortable in any setting, and where to take my seat, and how to hold my position no matter who is around and to always see myself just as valuable. Barbara has shown me over the years how to organize meetings, how to rally the troops, and how to set an atmosphere conducive to bring about change. These are valuable lessons I will never forget. She has taught me how to open my arms wide to embrace my sisters of all nationalities, and recognize and celebrate their lives and legacies. By example she has taught me how to never give up on my dreams and to fulfill my divine purpose on this earth. I have learned from her to have a desire to pour out every God-given thing I have to give to this life before it ends. Because her well runs deep, I know that I will be drawing wisdom and guidance from her for a very long time. Her mentorship has taught me that hard work and dedication brings great rewards. Her life speaks, "Don't talk about it… be about it!"

My message for all who read this book is this: look for the best good qualities in those who captivate you. Follow the steps they took to seeing manifested success, then do it better, and experience even greater results! With God all things are possible. Take shade under the trees bearing good fruit, partake of their revelation, insight, wisdom and clear understanding… there you'll be restored, there your rest will be pleasant.

Mathew 7:17 - Even so, every healthy (sound) tree bears good fruit (worthy of admiration) (Amp.)

Linda Morgan
Jazz Legacy Preservationist
A Life of Servanthood

Well today is a good day, a day I will call my own,
Because this is the day that I have taken a pause, to reap the seeds
that have been sown.
I've been asked by my friend, Barbara to be a part of her next book,
I am grateful for the opportunity,
I am allowed to take a closer look.
A look into my life as I have given to others,
a journey that has no end,
my life of servanthood, a life of being a mentor
or a lifelong friend.

As I thought about my story and the things that I wanted to say,
so many thoughts kept coming to mind, it is harder to do this way.
My gift of prose is my special gift that shows up
when I least expect it.
It just starts to pour itself on paper, sometimes
I'm amazed at what I get.
The Magic Of Mentoring, Pearls of Wisdom,
is the title that she has given,
why did my mind just draw a blank to try to rekindle,
What I've been living.

As I think about mentoring, being a mentee
or pouring your life into another soul,
I think about hearing the call from Susan Taylor,
that made me think that I was bold.
Bold enough to care for someone else,

bold enough to take a stance,
bold enough to reach out and seek Barbara's
friendship to take a closer glance.
I sought out Ms. Barbara, we made our 1st intro
at the Regalettes all white affair,
I paid my $100 because it was this friendship
with Barbara that I knew would be there.

We hit it off in the beginning, and I made her my big sister friend,
someone who 6 years later, I know that I can always depend.
She has taught me a lot about relationships,
she has made my life so full,
I always think of our first meeting, I was being vetted I feel,
and this was no bull.
She made sure I was someone she could help;
she made sure I was the real deal,
to be someone in her life up-close and personal,
you don't know how this feel.

I brought along my skills to help her launch the
L.A. CARES Mentoring Board,
not knowing all the time that our lives as sisters,
would eventually strike a cord.
A bond of mentoring that has lasted a few years,
totally built on trust,
one of the main ingredients in a mentoring relationship,
it is absolutely a must.
I now only have 2 older sisters, with whom this bond
has not been built,
I'm thankful for our friendship,
because it makes me feel no guilt.

I never had any concept on mentoring or playing
a special role in someone's life.

But I have spent the majority of my time here on earth,
being someone's wife.
Whether the relationships worked out for the best
or whether they all came to an end,
I must be a special type of person, that people can call their friend.
I believe that mentoring takes its own special course down the
winding road we travel,
uncovering new and fresh relationships are
always there to be unraveled.

I know that I mentor my children because it's a call,
you can't ignore,
you must show up for them at every moment,
your life is their open door.
A door that is never shut, a door that guides them most of the time,
helping them to shape their paths through life,
always giving your last dime.
I will always mentor my children, it's a calling that you can't
refuse.
From the moment of birth until their death,
a love that you can't abuse.

So to me, mentoring is a lifelong journey, that shows up as it will,
you make the best of it by cherishing it or something to fulfill.
Keep your heart open at all times,
and see where it might show you its true face
to help someone or to be somewhere and know
that you are in the right place.
To change the course of someone's life or make it just a bit better
this is the ending to my essay for the book, my open letter.

The Magic
of MENTORING
PEARLS of WISDOM

Section Two

Valerie Polk
Administrative Executive
HUMBLE BEGINNINGS

I am the only child, only granddaughter, only niece in my mother's family. My mother and father were divorced at an early age and most of my time was spent with my maternal grandmother in Luverne, Alabama, which is about 30 miles south of Montgomery. My mother worked two jobs, which caused her to be away in Montgomery. My grandmother was not only my role model, but also my mentor. She instilled all of the qualities that have molded me into the woman that I am today.

Growing up as a child in the small town of Luverne, with a population of about 10,000 in 1970, I spent most of my free time in the fields with my great-grandfather, who lived to be 104 years old. I can remember collecting the small coke bottles from around the neighborhood and trading them in for 50 cents, which was a lot of money back then. We would pick vegetables from the field and take them around to the homes of people who didn't have food. Listening to the stories of my great-grandfather about his parents and how he wanted to see me go to school, get an education, and not have to work in the fields, was the beginning of what would be my life's story.

During the summer months, my grandmother would take me to Montgomery to spend two weeks with my paternal grandparents. My grandmother always wanted to make sure that I knew both sides of my family. My father's mother was just as nurturing, always talking to me and giving me her wisdom on life. She had a group of friends that would come over every Friday to play cards. They had their little appetizers set up on the table and they always had some advice for all of the kids. Most of my cousins didn't want to hear it, but I would sit and soak up every word. A lot of times we don't take the time to talk to kids, we talk at them. In order to be an effective mentor, you have to be open to understand and speak to their situations. You must make them feel as though there is a light at the end of that tunnel and help guide them through it. My elders provided their wisdom to me, which has helped guide me through life.

During the summer of 1972, I was in Montgomery spending two weeks with my father's parents. My mother was getting married in a week, and we were spending time looking for her wedding dress and planning her wedding. Every day she would pick me up, and we would hang out for hours getting ready for this wedding. One week before the wedding, a tragedy struck. My mother's fiancé, who was getting ready for the wedding as well, was killed in a tragic accident by a drunk driver who ran his truck off the road between Selma and Montgomery, Alabama, five days before they were scheduled to walk down the aisle. My mother was devastated. The day before the funeral, we spent all day together. On the day of the funeral my mother picked me up. We had breakfast and went shopping. She dropped me off at my aunt's house, told me she loved me, and she would be back to pick me up after the funeral. I was expecting her around 6:00 or 7:00 p.m. that evening. She never showed up. The next day I woke up asking for her, but she was nowhere to be found. I did not know that would be the last time I would see my mother, but it was.

The series of events that occurred, I was told, began after the funeral as they left the cemetery. It was more than she could bear. My mother told someone that she was walking back to the cemetery, which was less than a mile from the house. She wasn't missed until about two hours later. When they looked for her, she had gone back to the cemetery and committed suicide.

I was 10 years old and my life was changed forever. I had not seen my father in a couple of years, but he showed up at my aunt's house a few days later. At this point, I still did not know my mother was gone. He took me for a ride and told me what had happened. I told him I wanted to go back to my grandmother's house in Luverne. Upon my arrival back in Luverne, my grandmother greeted me at the door and just held me in her arms. All I could hear her say was, "Baby it's going to be alright, this too shall pass." Preparations were made for my mother's home coming and a new chapter in my life started.

My grandmother had three friends, Mrs. Norma Jackson, Mrs. Bula Mapson and Mrs. Georgia. All three of these ladies, who were in their 60's and 70's, became not only my mother and my mentors, but they are, to this day, the lights that guide my path through life. My definition of a mentor started early on. My grandmother and the other ladies shared stories of wisdom and taught me how to keep my head up and allow God to lead my path.

I became a Sunday school teacher at an early age and my tragedy had now become my story and how I got over it. I will always remember Mrs. Brown saying, "Baby, life is a journey and it ain't easy, but if you let God lead your path, and when you get to that crossroad in life, He will point you in the right direction." A day never went by that one of those four ladies didn't part something into my spirit that follows me every day of my life. Even now when I feel that life is a struggle, I can hear those voices in my head as clear as if I was still sitting on that porch.

My grandmother was everything in the world to me. My friends would get angry, because all I wanted to do was stay in the house and cook with her. She was the town baker and worked for the Mayor. She made sure I went to school. We were in church every Sunday and all of the preachers came to our house for dinner after church. During the summer months it was a revival at someone's church and yes, we were there. She never met a stranger and fed many people that were less fortunate. On the weekends, my grandmother and I would ride through the housing projects and pick up kids, I would braid hair and my grandmother would give them clothes that had been donated by the people uptown. She is the reason that my heart smiles when I can be a positive light shining in someone else's life.

I can remember how clean my grandmother used to keep her house. We would visit her friends and I would find myself hanging clothes on the clothesline, dusting and cleaning for them. One day I asked my grandmother to call all of her friends and let them know that I would come to their house after school and help them around the house. I did not know how much these good deeds would change my life. After spending time with Mrs. Brown, Ms. Jackson, and Mrs. Georgia, I heard what they were saying. As kids you don't really think about it until later. They all brought something different and special and now that I am older, the stories of wisdom still resonate in my soul and have propelled me through many hard times.

Mentoring are the voices of the women that came before me, and the women that stand with me, and the women who have imparted wisdom that I hold dear to my heart. I can now share that wisdom and my life lessons with all of the children that touch my life on a daily basis. Every child deserves to have a positive messenger in their lives, someone that talks the talk and walks the walk with them."

I moved to Los Angeles, California, in June 1994 with my two daughters. Even though we think we know the path of this journey called life, there is always a hurdle thrown somewhere in the race. In 2000, I was stricken with an illness that caused me to leave my job. My first question was, "Why me?" You never know the plan that GOD has for you and it definitely wasn't mine. While sitting home feeling sorry for myself because I couldn't work, God had another plan. It started with my daughter who brought a friend home and asked if she could stay. My first response was, "We can't take care of her." My daughter's response was, "Mom, GOD will work it out and we have to help her." Her mother was an addict and her father was in prison. After making phone calls and getting assistance, she became a part of our family. She went on to finish high school and received a full scholarship to Cal State Northridge, graduating with honors. My daughter, now a senior in High School, wanted me to speak to all of the children in our community. We were now on a mission to make a difference in their lives.

Many girls and boys in the neighborhood would come to my house for rap sessions every Monday, Wednesday and Friday after school. We would talk about their lives, why they were doing what they were doing, and what we could do to change those things. On Saturdays, we would cook out in the park. I would sit for hours and help them with paperwork to get back into school. I would pretend to be someone's parent to get them the assistance that they needed. A lot of these children, especially the young men, were gang bangers and drug dealers with no one in their lives to direct them. I spent five years making a difference in their lives. Of the thirty plus kids that crossed my path and were part of my life during that season, I only lost three. One was killed in a car accident and two were killed in gang-related activities. A lot of the children went on and graduated from high school. Some were set in their ways and they wanted to know that they were loved and that someone saw past their faults. It's not always the conversations that you have with kids and young adults; it's that feeling of knowing that someone genuinely cares and loves them. I had become something that was missing in their lives and making a difference meant more than anything. I grew to love these kids as if they were my own, and to this day, 20 years later, I still hear from some of them.

In 2004, I met a phenomenal woman, Barbara Perkins. I watched her host meetings and give presentations. I wanted to be like her. A few years passed and our paths crossed again when she asked me to assist her with the Los Angeles Chapter of the National CARES Mentoring Movement founded by Ms. Susan L. Taylor. I was honored and excited to stretch my wings and work with other children around the City of Los Angeles. I had worked with Barbara for a couple of years at a Sistah Summit in Northern California where I had the pleasure of meeting Ms. Susan L. Taylor.

I had been talking about moving back to Atlanta, Georgia, to be closer to my father. Ms. Taylor and I had a conversation about a position in Atlanta as the National Director of the National CARES Mentoring Organization. I gladly accepted and things were moving forward with my relocation. I arrived in Atlanta in June 2008 with the goal of assisting Ms. Taylor and the CARES Organization with recruiting one million mentors. With the continued support of Barbara Perkins, we were well on our way. After my tenure with CARES, I continued to mentor young girls and boys on being all that they can be and there is no limit to what they can do. My main focus is on young adults, single mothers and single fathers. If I had to give some words of wisdom as it relates to mentoring, I would say mentoring can be the most rewarding thing you do for both the mentor and the mentee. Mentoring is, knowing that the message you are delivering is clear and concise and knowing the listener has clear understanding of the message being delivered.

In 2009, I met my husband Gregory Polk and together we blended our families. We have six children and six grandchildren. Mentoring is an everyday job for us with our children, and we are always striving to help them with life's challenges and ensuring them that they can accomplish anything when they put their mind to it, staying focused and on task. You will always have stumbling blocks, but you have to know that through GOD, anything is possible.

I have known Barbara for almost ten years, and I can't really find the words to describe her. In my life, she is the light at the end of my tunnel. She has sustained me with her strength when weakness was all I knew. She has walked with me through those times when I didn't think I would make it on my own. While working as the National Director for the CARES Mentoring Organization, she kept me grounded and focused on the reason why we were doing this work. I remember when I had my last surgery in 2007 and I thought my world was coming to an end. Nothing was going right, I had to move out of my house and I was in the middle of transitioning from California back to Atlanta. I talked to Barbara every morning and the words that she shared and the prayers that she prayed helped me through my days. Since returning to Atlanta, there have been times when I wasn't in a good place in my life and I needed to hear her voice.

As women, we look for that special woman, who can be that person in our lives, one who doesn't judge, and one, who doesn't always have an opinion, but will listen with open ears and allow you to talk and express what you're feeling. Barbara is that one. She's not just a mentor, she's my friend, my confidant, my sister, my angel, a shoulder to cry on when you're miles away, and she's that smile on the other end of the phone when you want to cry. Her words resonate long after she finishes speaking. She is my "Phenomenal Woman."

As I continue to go through this journey called life, I can look back and say, GOD has blessed me with many things and one of those things that I will forever cherish, be grateful for and hold dear to my heart is Mrs. Barbara Perkins. I lost my mother at the age of 10 but at the age of 50, He blessed me with a Real Life Angel. May GOD continue to bless her with the wisdom and the knowledge to continue to be all that she is and all that she will ever be in my life and the lives of all that she mentors.

I am a BLACK PEARL because I am a Blessed Miracle!

Juanita Palacios-Sims
Founder and Executive Director,
International Society of Black Latinos (ISBL)
Educating and Uniting
Our Communities

"Educating and Uniting Our Communities"

A mentor is an experienced and trusted adviser, a confidant, this according to Wikipedia. According to the Encyclopedia of Informal Education, "The classic definition of mentoring is of an older experienced guide who is acceptable to the young person and who can help ease the transition to adulthood by a mix of support and challenge. In this sense it is a developmental relationship in which the young person is inducted into the world of adulthood."

Mentoring for me is such a privilege. To be a trusted adviser and confidant to a younger person or anyone is an experience like no other and an honor. To be a mentor comes with its challenges. It is not always an easy job, but it is a rewarding one.

A few years ago, I joined a mentoring organization for young girls in Foster care. To tell you the truth, I don't remember how I found out about the organization or if someone had invited me to attend a meeting.

When I arrived at the orientation on an early Saturday morning, I found myself sitting beside a group of professional women eagerly waiting, like me, to be mentors. A young lady was standing in front of us welcoming and thanking the group for being there so early. She told us a little about herself, where she worked and when she joined the organization. She also talked to us about her journey in becoming a mentor and later a Mentor Director for the organization. The Director told us about her experiences with the young girls in foster care, for example, where some of them came from, and their backgrounds, which in most cases was not so pretty. It was explained that a lot of the girls were physically and sexually abused by family members or people that they knew. Some girls were taken from their parents/mothers because of drug abuse on the parent's part and placed into foster care. Other girls had been moved from one home to another, time and time again, with no stability in their lives. And there were a couple of girls whose families couldn't take care of them and their siblings.

The more I listened to the stories of each girl, the more I was anxious to be a mentor, a savior to one or more of the girls. In my mind, I had a day or two in the month to meet with her, take her out to dinner or a movie, and buy her a few things. More and more, I was excited to be a part of a girl's life. Little did I know what was coming ahead!

Then reality set in. The Director asked us if we could commit a year to spend with a foster girl. Were we willing to talk to them at least three times a week, two weekends out of the month and most importantly, keep up with their grades? She told us that some of the girls did not have stability or a stable person in their lives. Some of them were moved around so much that if they had established a close relationship with a caregiver, a friend or a teacher, they were suddenly placed somewhere else and there went that relationship. And then there were a couple of the girls, blessed to have loving grandparents (mostly a grandmother) as a caregiver.

There was the "trust" issue. Most of the girls did not trust anyone. They had been let down so many times that the best way for them to handle things was to keep to themselves and not let anyone into their space. I started thinking more and more about what the Director was telling us. Did I really have that kind of time? Did I really want to get involved? Did I really have the energy to put into mentoring? Was I someone that could really change a person's path?

Finally we were given an option. We were told that in order to be a mentor, there was going to be a training period of seven to eight months before we met and were matched with a girl. Once a month on Saturday mornings we would have to go to the Center for training. We had to be fingerprinted and answer a lot of questions in order for us to qualify and move forward. The training would give us a chance to decide if we wanted to continue to be a mentor and it would prepare us for the union with the girls. I did it! I went through the program and decided that I would help in mentoring a young girl. I would make the time, get involved, and put the energy needed to help someone.

The mentor's graduation day finally arrived and we were introduced to our mentees. It was like being pregnant and finally having a baby, but in this case she was already a teen. When I was finally connected with my mentee it was great! The day I met my first mentee is the day I will never forget. She was sixteen, beautiful, and full of life. This was the same person who at fifteen years of age gave her mother an ultimatum to leave the drugs or she and her brother would leave her. Needless to say, she contacted a social worker and a few months later they were placed in different foster homes.

This beautiful young lady had been in the organization for a year or two before my arrival. She had a mentor whom she had been close to before she moved out of the state. They continued their relationship, but after a while it became hard for them to have an effective one, so it faded away.

It has been a joy being a mentor. Mentoring is a beautiful and important gift. I really enjoy the time I spent and currently spend with my mentees (I have a couple of mentees). Through tears, laughter, homework, checking teachers and counselors and making sure I am giving her what she needs has been an adventure for both of us.

She is not the only person that is getting something out of this, I am learning a great deal from her as well. In my life, God has put so many young people in my path. As I walk through it, I try to give a word or two of encouragement to young people, even if I don't know them.

As a mentor, I realize how many young people look for a word or two to give them hope, a hug to get them through the day, or just a nice word from someone to make them feel loved or even noticed.

Although I did not have a direct mentor in my life growing up, I had many women to look up to that helped shape my life; my very own mother, grandmother, aunts, women in the church, and teachers/councilors. It took a village and I believe that it still takes a village.

I would wake up in the mornings and go to my mami's room to give her a kiss "good morning" and she would be on her knees praying for me, for us, her children. I would go give her a goodnight kiss and she would be reading her Bible or on her knees thanking the Lord for my return. It was that example of a woman and much more that made me the woman I am today.

My 6th grade teacher was Mrs. Gain. She was a beautiful woman and very strict. She did not play. She was someone that I respected and looked up to. Mrs. Gain knew my potential, even when I didn't. She would stay on me and make sure I completed my homework and would keep me after school when my work was not done. One day I asked her if she liked me, because I felt that she was always picking on me. She replied that not only did she like me, that she wanted to make sure that I kept my grades up because she felt that I was smart. I remember how that made me feel. My "mean" teacher thought I was smart. Today I think of her often and I am so thankful that she was in my life.

My Tia Maria Victor is another woman that has had a big influence in my life, even up to this day. Although she is no longer with us, her words of encouragement still whisper in my ears.

As I walk through this life, I am grateful to have been blessed by both men and women that have encouraged me, including my husband, Tia Gladys, Barbara Perkins, Darrell Brown, Jason Seward, Mrs. Vera, Mrs. Ferguson and so many more. I am thankful today for the people in my life, and as I continue to walk on this earth, I will do my best to encourage a child and be a mentor.

Avis Jones-DeWeever, Ph.D.
Leadership & Personal Development Coach
Connecting the Generations Through
Mentoring

At heart, I'm still a country girl who knows what it feels like to have the hot rays of the summer sun beating down on the back of my neck in a remote, dusty, Virginia tobacco field. A girl who spent long days with the cool sensation of dirt between my toes, and feeling the gooey texture of freshly made mud pies, while anxiously awaiting the critical gaze of my mother's discerning eye. I lived a happy and simple childhood. If someone had told me then that this small-town girl would one day build a career that would allow her to travel the world, engage in frequent contact with the White House, and even participate in high-level meetings with the President of the Unites States himself, I would have not believed it possible. But you see, all of that is the beauty of mentors. Those precious souls that come about and see something in you, something that you fail to even see in yourself and then they go further. They pour into you their time, their wisdom, and their expertise so that you may refine your gift, mold it, build it, and then one day, before you know it, you're ready to soar.

I've been fortunate to have a lifetime full of mentors. Even today, I marvel at those who continue to guide me, advise me, and believe in me, even in times of turmoil or potential difficulty. But my first, my dearest, and by far my most impactful mentor was also a country girl, who also grew up with dirt between her toes. Still she gave me all that she could until the day of her very last breath. My dear grandmother, Ada Alexander Reid, was really more than a grandmother to me. She would be more accurately described as a second mother. You see, my family and I lived with her as part of a deal my father brokered with her in exchange for my mother's hand. And so, every day while my parents were off at work and my much older sister was off to school, it was just me and grandma, fishing in the nearby pond, collecting vegetables in the family garden, or completing any of the dozens of tasks that are necessary to keep a family running smoothly. I simply adored her, not just because she was my grandmother, but because of intimate knowledge of who she was as a person. You see, my grandmother was a fighter. She was not one to be intimidated by others, no matter the adversary. She always carried a straight spine, had a sharp mind and a fierce wit, which she used when necessary to make piercing and moving arguments at the drop of a dime. She was fiercely proud of Black people, our power and our potential, and she refused to sit still for injustice; even in the days when doing so might very well bring an end to her life.

I can't remember when I first heard the story about one of the ways my grandparents fought back against the evils of segregation in their small Virginia town. At a time when not only schooling was segregated, but transportation to school was non-existent for Black children, my grandparents refused to merely allow their children to walk for miles back and forth to school each day while white children rode by, taunting them on school buses that my grandparents and countless other Black Virginia families in part financed through their tax dollars. So they decided to do something about it. They gathered the other Black parents in the community, they pooled their money, and they bought a bus. They then took turns driving that bus to ensure their children got to and from school safely each day. It was just this sort of determination, creativity and courage that I saw in her character each and every day that we spent together. It was those qualities that she breathed into me early on, even as an adoring child.

By the time I went to college I thought I knew with confidence what it was I wanted to be. My mind was made up. A future as a civil rights attorney was all but certain. So, when I attended a career fair during my senior year at my beloved Virginia State University, it was admittedly an activity I embarked upon much more to fill time and socialize than to truly explore new possibilities for a future career path. While there, I stumbled across a very enthusiastic graduate school recruiter. I told him quite matter-of-factly, law school was in the cards for me, not graduate school. But his offer of a waived application fee and the potential of thousands of dollars in graduate school funding was enough for me to take notice and explore the possibility of a plan B. Good thing I did, too, because when faced with the choice of incurring six-figures in law-school debt, versus receiving a full scholarship plus a monthly stipend to attend graduate school, I gladly took option B, with the original plan of delaying, but not ending my law school aspirations.

Fate, it seems, had other plans. I found I enjoyed the challenge that graduate education provided, and so upon completing my Master's degree, I decided to look into the opportunities that Doctoral studies would provide. It was through this process that I happened upon my next trajectory-changing mentor. Her name was Dr. Linda Williams. She was a true scholar/practitioner in the field of political science. Never one to be limited by the four walls of a college classroom, she was a respected scholar, activist, and author. She proved that it was possible to be building a career that weaved in and out of academia, and one that didn't require a watering down of movement-building activity. I needed to see her, a Black woman, making her own way in a male-dominated, and frankly, white male dominated academic profession, but doing it on her own terms, and in her own way to know that it was possible. I had to see her, to see the future me. And so, with her prodding, when it came time to make a decision about where I would go for my Doctoral studies, the choice was clear. I wanted to mold my abilities and model my career after someone who had become a fierce advocate on behalf of the social, economic, and political empowerment of Black people. And under her wing, and with her guidance, I turned that aspiration into a lived reality.

In the professional arena I've had the touch of several mentors along the way. Not all of them looked like me, but each challenged me, pushed me, held me to high standards, and gave me the feedback I needed to grow. However, perhaps none was more impactful than the legendary Dr. Dorothy Height. I remember the first day we met as if it was yesterday. I had been tapped to potentially becoming the Director of the National Council of Negro Women's Research, Public Policy and Information Center, a new think-tank style division of the organization to be focused exclusively on the condition of African American women. It was a dream job that gave me the opportunity to finally focus on my particular concern for the lives and life chances of Black women exclusively. Dr. Height was to be my final interview for the position. It's quite intimidating to be in a room with greatness. To know I was meeting an icon who had long fought on the battlefields for both race and gender justice, was humbling indeed. But as soon as I saw her, it was something about her eyes that reminded me of my grandmother. I knew from that moment on we would connect and that we did. I worked with her from that day until virtually her last. Her grace, her dignity, her intellect, and her high standards were all qualities that I sought to embody. Having those last precious years working with her, left an imprint on me that I still wear proudly to this day, and it is through her that I got to know so many other greats, who have touched my life, lifted me, molded me, advised me as I came into my own during my critical years, and ultimately becoming the youngest ever Executive Director of NCNW.

Melanie Campbell, who served as co-Convener of the Black Women's Roundtable along with Dr. Height became and still is a critical advisor for my career development. She ultimately became one of my first clients when I started my own consulting firm, proving that she believed in me by not just words, but through actions. It was through Mrs. Height's connection, that my life first became entangled with Barbara Perkins.

When I think about our relationship, I think of Barbara as being less of a mentor and more of a Fairy Godmother of sorts. She has the ability to cut right through and pull the best visions out of me. Not only was she a key advisor to navigating the generational challenges I faced at times during my tenure at NCNW, but also as I transitioned to entrepreneurship, she helped with my growth and evolution as an entrepreneur. It was her faith in my ability that helped me to respect the tug I was feeling to expand my expertise into the areas of executive and personal development coaching, and for that I will be forever grateful.

As important as mentorship has been for me, I have worked to pay it forward in the lives of others that have crossed my path along the way. And through this process I have found that our young people are yearning for our wisdom. They thirst for our time, and they crave a connection with those who have gone before them. In short, they need us. But this need is not a one-way street. The most closely held secret of mentorship is that it can be at least as beneficial for the mentor as it is for the mentee. And I don't mean the "oh, it just feels so good to help someone" benefits, even though this is very much the case. But there are very practical, discernable benefits to connecting with and truly engaging young people that are both personally and professionally beneficial. The energy, creativity, unique perspective, and social media savvy of mentees have enhanced my career in a variety of very tangible ways. And so, when I think of mentoring relationships I think of mutually beneficial partnerships that entail an exchange of ideas, aspirations, connections and gifts based on a solid foundation of friendship and mutual respect.

This is the brilliance of mentoring. It is the connecting of generations. It is the collection and exchange of wisdom. It is the human connection and the commitment to live the challenge espoused by Mary Church Terrell to "lift as we climb." It is reciprocity in action and it is a joy.

Jacqueline Castillo
President, Legacy Ladies, Inc.
MENTORING IS NOT ABOUT SELF

"You can be anything you want to be, just put your mind to it." Those were the words I heard in my home while growing up. I often reflect on my path to adulthood. My mother was the person always there to guide and encourage me to be the best that I can be. Mother was a woman of faith and strength. The most important lesson she taught me was to give back to the community. She made sure I understood how blessed I was and how much God had provided for me.

I remember the days when mother would take my sister and me to NAACP meetings. She helped us to understand that even children could fight for injustice. She helped us to understand that leadership comes in all shapes and sizes. She told us that leadership skills were important skills to have and that leadership skills were required to get the job of fighting for injustice done.

Growing up in an average family of humble beginnings, I remember the tremendous amount of love that I felt coming from my mother to us and to others who were in need of a helping hand. Mother was that consistent role model in my life. She was my mentor then and at 93 years old, she continues to hold that special place in my life.

Mentoring is so very important to me. It is heartbreaking to see the state of affairs for young Black girls in communities across the nation. There is a desperate need for role models and mentors to be matched with these young ladies.

Mentoring can make the overall positive difference in communities where Black girls are at disproportionate risk for a life of limited opportunities. Mentoring Black girls through the maze of personal challenges that are sure to show up in their lives, as my mother provided for me, is critical, which is why I am such an advocate for mentoring in our communities.

As President of Legacy Ladies, Inc., a non-profit organization, I have focused on three high schools in Los Angeles to provide a mentorship program through an afterschool program called, *From the School House to The White House Leadership Program*. The focus is on high school girls in disadvantaged communities, living in foster homes or single-family households.

Whenever I am able to walk the halls of some of the schools we target, it becomes even clearer to me that this is my mission in life. When I look into the eyes of young girls on campuses around Los Angeles, I am often filled with sadness and pain for some of them. These experiences serve as motivators for me to share my story and coach them on the issue of leadership.

The many personal stories of the girls in our afterschool program have touched my heart. Some stories, more than others, become the ones you might identify with or feel sensitive to. One such story shared by a special teenage girl who I would call Celeste captured my attention and frankly my heart. The dysfunctional house and the mental illness of both parents made life very difficult for this family. Her mother left an abusive heterosexual relationship for a complex lesbian relationship.

Eventually, Celeste became homeless and moved from one relative's house to another. Through encouragement she received by being in the mentoring program and with the coaching and confidence shown to her, Celeste began to gain self-esteem.

She began to dream and grow her vision beyond her current circumstances. She knew that through Legacy Ladies leadership program she would have help.

Today, Celeste is a first-year college student and wants to become a neurologist. She understands the circumstances of her life with her mother and has released the animosity perhaps she once had. Celeste's focus is on completing her studies and she is on a career path towards success in the medical profession.

I thank my mother for being the best role model and mentor I could have. I also would like to thank Barbara A. Perkins for the opportunity to share my story among the other very impressive stories. Barbara sets an example for how we should work together to meet our children where they are. She is a true community champion who sets the bar high for those in service to our children. She believes that all of our children deserve the very best.

Juanita Holcombe Hamilton
Corporate Trainer and Business Consultant
A Resource and A Challenge

I met Barbara Perkins along my journey to help others. At the time, she was a leader for the Los Angeles region of a national mentor-recruitment effort. We connected because of our shared commitment and passion for mentoring the young and uplifting underserved communities.

There were many folks that touched my life in profound ways. For that, I am now and will be forever grateful. My mother and father were my primary mentors. My family members, teachers, and friends were also important mentors. I would be remiss if I did not acknowledge the key gift that my father gave to me. Daddy treated me like a Princess. He encouraged me to recite the Pledge of Allegiance and the twenty-third Psalm at every family gathering. Sometimes I would act a little shy, but he gave me the "look" that meant, "You are special, come to the front and show everybody what you have learned."

My daddy helped me develop my self-confidence. He was a well-dressed, dark, chocolate brown-skinned farm boy with very white beautiful straight teeth. I was blessed with his white teeth and dark skin. I always knew that "Black was beautiful." Daddy taught me the value of every person. He often brought home a lonely man from work or the community that needed a hot meal and a clean shave. I learned the importance of checking on the elders just in case they needed help with watering the lawn or bringing something from the store. I was shown respect and in turn tried very hard to show that to others.

My mother was a stay-at-home mom and took special care of six children and a husband every day. Breakfast was always served hot during school days. My hair was always combed and braided, and I wore ribbons every day. On Easter Sunday, I wore my hair down. This was a special treat because the Saturday before Easter, mama would hot press all the girls' hair and daddy would cut the boys' hair. I am amazed by how much energy they put forth to ensure six children were raised with love and affection.

We went to church and enjoyed the hunt for Easter eggs. At Christmas we helped decorate the Christmas tree. We did all the traditional things and even the non-traditional. We had friends who were wealthy and friends who were on county welfare. We had fun with everybody. We had a formal Sunday dinner every week. We all had our special seat at the table. Of course we argued if someone sat in someone else's chair. During the week dinner was ready when daddy came home. His bath water was hot in the tub and when he emerged clean and handsome from a hard day at the factory that was our cue to sit down at the table.

I learned to cook by being close to mother. She allowed me to peel the potatoes; clean the greens, wash the beans, and husk the corn. It's funny that some of my friends seem surprised when they learn that I am a pretty good cook.

I treasure the many summers spent down on my paternal grandparents' farm in Alabama, and at my maternal grandfather's church. We also had a large garden in the city that we worked every summer. I was a Girl Scout, and learned a lot about survival skills and getting along with others. I do not fear getting my hands dirty. It's just that I don't like to keep them dirty! I love to cook and to entertain family and friends. My folks always had someone different at the dinner table. The conversations were interesting and the topics covered everything from politics, business to community affairs, family problems and gossip.

I was taught by example from all sides of my family that all are welcome and nobody goes away hungry. When someone got into trouble, my parents did not hide it from us. They taught us that there were consequences for one's actions. "You can learn something from a fool, if only how not be one."

My daddy died when I was 14 years of age. He had a faulty heart valve that the doctors could not repair. Today, his condition is commonly repaired with microsurgery. His passing was devastating to us all. I took it very hard. Many nights I laid awake hoping and praying that it was a mistake, and that he would be walking up the stairs any day. He never came back, but my memory of him never left and lives in my heart forever.

I learned about the loss of a loved one and to value the precious time we have together. I think that is why I choose to hold onto my friendships so dearly. I try to find the good in most people and situations.

My mother was left to raise six children to the best of her ability. She did not go out to work for at least a year after my daddy died. She was organized and we never missed a meal. She rented out a small house on our property and befriended the new tenant who also had children. They started a sewing circle, and she made many of my dresses and my sister's dresses for several years. I still remember the beautiful red, green and blue jumpers and bright white blouses. Today my closets are filled with colorful clothes, hats, scarves and jewelry, influenced by the clothes my mother would make.

I learned to be resourceful. I learned how to choose patterns, cut fabric, thread a needle, and use a thimble. My paternal grandmother was a fabulous quilter. I learned the basics and look forward to making something special someday in memory of all the ladies that taught me to sew and dress like a lady.

In school I had several great teachers. Mrs. Brown was my freshman homeroom teacher. She knew that I had lost my father the summer before school began. She would offer me special assignments and hired me to do babysitting for her on the weekends. I earned extra money and she was a wonderful example of teacher, trainer and friend. We talked and laughed and became good friends over the years. I was introduced to her friends who also mentored me.

Mrs. Fletcher worked in the attendance office and she selected me to work with her for extra credit. I learned office skills and worked well with adults and students. I took speech classes and learned about debate and drama. I had the lead in plays in both sophomore and junior years. I was elected Recording Secretary of the Student Council. I loved school and was a very good student. Mr. Giovanni was my geography teacher and he introduced me to the world of politics. I volunteered to work on the congressional campaign of Congressman Charles Whalen (R) Ohio. I learned about the differences in philosophy between Democrats and Republicans. I learned to vote for the person and the issues and not solely the party.

I attended college in Ohio and California, majoring in Business Administration and Business Management. I continue to learn as I consider it a lifelong pursuit. I am a corporate trainer, business consultant and mediator.

The church ladies from Shiloh set the standard for lady-like behavior. They sang in the choir or stood by the door. They visited the sick and the shut-ins and provided benevolent care to those in need. They wore fancy hats and beautiful clothes with matching handbags, gloves and shoes. They corrected us when we were too loud and gave encouragement when we needed to speak up. If we wore miniskirts too short they would raise an eyebrow and let us know, "Honey, that is not appropriate for church." When someone got pregnant before marriage, they were sheltered and provided guidance. We rarely made the same mistakes. All children were loved.

All of these experiences taught me how to be a mentor, most importantly to my own daughter, for 30 years. As a community service worker, it is my honor to work with the youth at Job Corp and Girls Inc. I also work closely as the Community Development Director for my church. Barbara Perkins and I have worked together to bring formal mentoring to several churches in the African American Episcopal Church. I pray that I have been an example and a resource to the people I have encountered on this wonderful and challenging journey of life

Cynthia Mitchell Heard
Vice President of Communications and Advocacy
My Story: My Humble Mentor

"Tell me and I forget, teach me and I may remember,
involve me and I learn." Benjamin Franklin

Over the past twenty-four years, I have been an intricate partner in the field of Social Services. Since 1989, I have worked diligently to facilitate social changes within at-risk communities throughout Los Angeles County and across America. During those several decades, I have assisted in helping to build collaborative child welfare, educational partnerships and innovative continuums, focusing on at risk and Foster youth throughout Los Angeles. Thank you to the amazing leader, Congresswoman Karen Bass. My primary focus was to develop and structure local academic and life-skill mentoring models, which were replicable and could demonstrate success and innovation.

As a key advocate and a pioneer leader I assisted with building these social service youth and family models that included Los Angeles County Family Preservation and Wrap Around, Family Support Programs Models, as well as many other innovative models across the United States. I am most proud of the collaborative partnerships and efforts to work together with the Department of Children and Family Services Probation and Inter-Agency Council on Child Abuse and Neglect, to design a unique "Mentoring Best Practices Model" called, The Los Angeles County Community Based Mentoring, serving only foster and probation youth in Los Angeles County.

Thank you for the amazing leadership of Deanne Tilton, ICAN and DCFS partners.

In 2003, I decided that I wanted to go to the root of the issue, so I joined forces with Children Uniting Nations as the Vice President of Programs, building community advocacy, national agendas/strategies, social services, collaborative partnerships, and programmatic support for at-risk and foster youth in America. Our programs focused on mentoring, recruitment and programs such as school-based academic and community. As an educational visionary, Dr. Victoria Stevens designed and created a "state of the art" Academic Educational Center for Children Uniting Nations.

You see, I believe that youth mentoring connects young people with responsible adults willing to commit their time to expose the youth to a different way of life. The outcome of this amazing relationship is often reduction of truancy, improved grades, and reduction of youth crime. Over the many decades, families, schools, and neighborhoods have been the foundation of support for youth in the past; however, the landscape of our communities has changed as well as the absence of traditional families (two-parent homes). The necessity has arisen for all to come together to fill in the gaps and give back to those youths that need a voice of reason, a helping hand, a shoulder to cry on, and unconditional guidance, in other words, a MENTOR.

My Story: My Humble Mentor

As a young child, I look back and remember the mentors that helped shape and guide my life in order for me to be the woman I have become today. It all started with a beautiful, heavy-set, stylish woman named, Bernice Crouch Hubbard, my "aunt Bernice". She was a strong, God-loving and family-driven woman. Through her dedication to family and legacy, she took care of my father from the age of 8 years after my grandmother passed away. So needless to say, Aunt Bernice was really my paternal grandmother.

In my early years, around the age of six, Aunt Bernice began to teach me the values of "unconditional" love, family, honesty, loyalty and respect. As a faithful woman of God, aunt Bernice would pick me up every Sunday morning, rain or shine, and drive us down to South Central, Los Angeles to attend church faithfully on Central Ave. A church founded and pastored by her husband, my uncle, Pastor Joseph Hubbard. The church is where she began her life lessons with me, teaching me to always keep God first in my life and the rest would follow. To this day, I reflect and model her faithful teachings and guidance.

Aunt Bernice and I were kindred spirits. She taught me that Sundays was for worship. Some weekends she would take me to the cleaners she owned on Central Ave. At the cleaners, she taught me how to work hard. She said it was a requirement for success. Her life was an example of leadership. She would say to me often, "You are a leader. You are strong and you are beautiful."

At the time, her words did not mean much to me, but as I began to mature into my teens and then into college years, I began to look in the mirror, see the reflection and the meaning of the words she would say to me daily. Aunt Bernice remained my confidant, my teacher and my guide. She recently died at age 97, but the memories of her laughter and wisdom will live forever with me.

Mentoring today for me is giving to others a sampling of what aunt Bernice gave to me. The lessons learned in that relationship are the same lessons I attempt to teach as a mentor to others. This is the beauty of mentoring. It does not have to be complicated at all. It is a dedication to someone else that is filled with a purposeful intention of helping them be better and do better.

I began mentoring shortly after graduate school. As a mentor, I try to be the example of what I speak about. I am most led to those who may not have enough or who are considered the underserved. I believe that EVERY child needs guidance and someone to take their hand. My life was a life of privilege. My parents were able to provide a worry-free academic life for all of their children. Everything we needed for school was provided. We only had to show up and be good students. This is not the case for so many young people deserving an education and wanting to attend college.

For me, giving back in the form of mentoring is not optional. It honors the memory of my dear aunt Bernice and respects the legacy of my parents. The personal benefits of mentoring and helping others are a satisfaction I find difficult to explain, at times it feels like the only thing I was put on this earth to do. I do not give to get back, but I have gotten back so much joy from helping others reach their goals in life. Working with children in the Foster system and often considered the forgotten ones, is where my passion is.

There is much more to do in communities across America, but if we each can help one child do well, succeed to their highest potential by avoiding the many pitfalls including a life of crime and other negative distractions, then our greatest work on earth will be done!

Elsie L. Scott, Ph.D.
Director, Ron Walters Leadership & Policy Center, Howard University
Mentoring Individual Needs

Some people decide they need a mentor and they seek and find someone who is successful in their particular field or interest area. Others see a person they admire, and they ask that person to be their mentor. I did not grow up knowing what a mentor was, so I did not seek out mentors early in my career. I grew up with the notion that if you were smart and could demonstrate that you had the appropriate skills and abilities to do a particular job, you would receive the job or assignment unless the person was prejudiced against you.

I excelled in grade school and was salutatorian of my high school class. I went to college thinking that I would become the lawyer that my father wanted me to be. Except for biology, I did well in my classes and even had time to help other students with their writing and research projects. There was no need for a mentor to get through undergraduate or law school - or so I thought.

Life is strange, because a person can be placed in your life that you do not seek out or know that you need. That is what happened to me during the first semester of my sophomore year at Southern University. Being the daughter of a prominent local leader made me value anonymity. I was able to walk around the campus and have no one stop me and ask me if I were one of Rev. Scott's daughters. The anonymity ended when I was called into the political science chairwoman's office one day. She asked me why I had not told her I was Rev. Scott's daughter. I had no idea that she knew my father. From that day until she died in August 2014, Dr. Jewel Limar Prestage was my mentor. Dr. Prestage took me under her tutelage and charted the course of my future. Even though she admired and respected my father, she encouraged me to pursue a Ph.D. instead of a law degree, and she started steering me in that direction. She also decided that I should follow in her footsteps by receiving my Ph.D. from the University of Iowa. She had been the first African American woman to receive a Ph.D. in Political Science from Iowa. She helped me obtain a financial package to support my graduate studies. She called key professors to let them know I was coming and to ask them to help me in my transition from undergraduate school and from a predominantly black university to a predominantly white university.

The uniqueness of Dr. Prestage stemmed from her approach to mentoring. I was not singled out for mentorship. She was constantly identifying students with potential, and guiding them in terms of their course of study, getting them exposed to opportunities outside the campus, helping them obtain financial assistance, and connecting them with people who could help them. She looked at each individual and tried to guide that person to the career pattern that she thought would work best for her or him.

She chose to teach at Historically Black Colleges and Universities (HBCUs) because there was a greater need, and she knew she could make a difference. Even though her teaching career was exclusively at HBCUs, she knew and was known by the "mainstream" political scientists. She was elected to leadership positions in predominantly white professional organizations, and she founded the Black Political Science Professional Association. She used connections made through her networks to help us gain admission to "majority" institutions and to secure fellowships and other financial support.

My tenure at Iowa was not smooth, but Dr. Prestage was always there pushing me to not give up. She would call my professors to see what they could do to help me acclimate to the environment. With her assistance, I was awarded a full fellowship, my second year that allowed me to focus full-time on my studies without having to work as a teaching assistant. I chose to leave Iowa after my second year because I needed to connect more with my black culture. She was not happy about me dropping out, but after I secured a fellowship and enrolled in a Ph.D. program headed by one of her former students, she did not try to convince me to go back to Iowa.

Throughout my professional career, Jewel Prestage has been there asking me to mentor her students who came after me, inviting me to speak to her students, recommending me for awards and honors, getting articles written about me and just being there for advice, counsel and support. After she died, many of her former students compared stories about her mentorship. Many of us had similar stories: we had come from rural environments; Jewel had identified our potential early in our undergraduate education; she had exposed us to people and opportunities that broadened our horizons; she introduced us to her former students who came before and after us; she would periodically call to check on us, our families and our careers; and she was one of our biggest cheerleaders. I did not initially see what she was doing as mentoring because her approach was similar to my mother's approach to mothering. Once the term mentoring, became popular, I recognized that what Jewel Prestage was doing was mentoring.

Another mentor who selected me and who has had a big impact on my life is Dr. Lee P. Brown. I had the opportunity to chair a panel on the police when I was in graduate school. One of the persons on the panel was Dr. Brown, who was the first African American to earn a Ph.D. in Criminology from the University of California, Berkeley. There were people in the audience who were disruptive and not respectful of the presenters. I was determined that the presenters would be able to make their presentations, so I did what I could to keep control of the session. Dr. Brown was impressed with how I handled the session, and as a result he became one of my mentors.

Periodically, he would call to find out how I was progressing in my career and I would see him at various professional meetings and events. He offered advice to me when I was Executive Director of the National Organization of Black Law Enforcement Executives (NOBLE). When Mayor David Dinkins appointed him Police

Commissioner for the City of New York, he offered me a deputy commissioner position. I initially rejected the offer because I had no interest in working inside a police department. I felt that it would be a step backward to work for a police department after I had earned a Ph.D. I eventually accepted the position, because my mentor convinced me that the position was a good career move. I never regretted taking the position, because I learned so much and gained new skills, contacts and friends.

I learned from Lee Brown how to listen and have an impact. In our executive staff meetings, he would let everybody have their say before he gave his opinion or decision on a particular issue. He was learning about his staff and forcing us not to be "me-to" followers of the boss. He also taught me how to support my staff when they got into trouble. I had a media crisis while he was out of the country. By the time he returned, there were many calls for my ouster. When I was summoned to his office, I came prepared to be fired or to resign. The first thing he did was to offer me a seat and asked me how I was doing. Secondly, he said, "Let's discuss how we will get passed this crisis." His support did so much to boost my morale and build my strength to handle crises instead of throwing in the towel.

Unlike Dr. Prestage, most of my positions have been somewhat short in tenure - three to five years. Therefore, a number of my mentees have been young people that I have met at conferences or seminars. They are not students that I may have a daily influence on their lives, rather they are persons who may be in positions where there is no one like me in their workplace or at their university. I receive calls or emails from people I do not know asking me to serve as their mentor. Unlike my generation, many young people select their mentors as opposed to being selected as I was. I am more likely to communicate with my mentees by email, text or Facebook, rather than face-to-face meetings.

The first time someone approached me and asked me to be their mentor, I had just turned 40. I took a slight offense because I was thinking that I was not old enough to be their mentor. I had assisted my students with internships, job and career opportunities, but at that time, I did not consider myself a mentor - I was just doing what college professors do, especially African American professors. After being approached by this young man, I realized that people younger than me were observing me, and they were viewing me as a role model from whom they could learn.

During my tenure with the New York City Police Department, I was able to mentor younger officers, especially women, black and Puerto Rican officers and civilian personnel. Even though I had not been a police officer, I was able to coach and advise officers on career paths within and outside the department. I spent time with the women helping them understand how to navigate a male-dominated profession. Because the scholarship programs came under my command, I was able to help officers prepare their applications. I worked with the female command officers, arranging opportunities for them to interact with women business executives to learn business management skills and promotional navigation skills. Some of my mentoring was deliberate and direct, but some was more leading and teaching by example. I knew that since I was one of the few women in a leadership position, women in the department saw me as a role model, and as such were modeling my dress, management and leadership styles.

At the Congressional Black Caucus Foundation, much of my mentoring was focused on the interns and fellows. I did not have daily contact with them because they had assignments on Capitol Hill and other government agencies. When I interacted with them, I tried to connect with them as individuals. I told them I was available to assist them after the program was over. I periodically reached out to some of them with whom I had developed a relationship, and others reached out to me for assistance with career advice, assistance in finding jobs or getting into graduate school.

Professional black women must go out of their way to mentor young black women. Some smart, but shy young women may be left behind because they are not assertive enough to approach a potential mentor. I was one of those smart, shy young women who excelled in school, but would never approach an accomplished person and ask for help. We must stop ignoring and dismissing the timid ones, because they are not in our faces, and they are not demanding that we help them as some of the more assertive young women are doing. Like Jewel Prestage and Lee Brown, we must recognize potential and help to groom the next generation of leaders.

I was fortunate to attend a HBCU where there was value in personal contact and where a master mentor was a department chairperson. I have been influenced by my mentors to see mentoring as coaching, teaching, sponsoring, parenting, leading, directing, listening, advising, supporting, and offering tough love. I have learned that mentoring cannot be a one-size-fits-all; it must be customized to the individual mentee. Some mentees will only be in your life for a season or a specific reason. You will help them though a particular crisis or phase of life, and they will move on to other mentors who have more of the resources they need for success. Other mentees will be in situations where you have to call in other mentors and sponsors to help them. Still other mentees will be with you for a lifetime, becoming so close that they will be like family.

I thank Barbara Perkins for inviting me to write this essay on mentoring. I met Barbara through my work with the Congressional Black Caucus Foundation. I remember her approaching me about helping her get the young women she was working with engaged in the Annual Legislative Conference. I was so impressed with what she was doing that I worked with her to not only have them attend the workshops, but to attend the Awards dinner also. Barbara felt that the young people would benefit from being in the room with the movers and shakers for various sectors of the black community. Since that time, I have been fortunate to work with her through the Black Women's Roundtable and to travel with her to Ghana to plan an international women's empowerment conference.

Rev. Deborah Chinaza Lee
Minister
My First and Best Mentor

I was my mother's 'trouble' child; at least that is how she has come to describe me on the few occasions that she has publically introduced me. Looking back, I can't really argue the point. It is not that I got into trouble often, but when I did, it normally had something to do with my mouth and my reliance on intellect and reason. Basically, I was a smart, know-it-all kid who did not know that I did not know it all.

I know there were times when my approach amazed my mother. She often attributed my way of being to my father, Gregory Lee. He is a very intelligent and practical man, so I can understand why she had that thought. Little did she know, it was also her support, encouragement, intelligence and most of all her heart, which had a big influence on my day-to-day movements.

As a matter of fact, I was known to watch my mother's every move. At times, I had to be pried from under her arm or chastised to leave the room during grown folk's conversations. "Can you just let your mother breathe?" is a comment that I heard quite frequently. But for me, every moment with her was a moment to learn and grow. I believed that the sun rose and set on my mother and I just wanted to be in the warmth.

When I was about seven years old, my aunt decided to take my older sister to get her ears pierced. I was not included simply because I was too young. Of course I disagreed and wrote my mother a letter explaining my readiness and maturity to be included. My mother was so undone by my effort and argument that she agreed to let me go. Little did she realize that watching her create correspondence and address individual concerns gave me the idea in the first place.

Despite the predicaments this attitude often got me in, my mother always encouraged me to stand, respectfully of course, for what I believed in. Even when I sent the third letter to the principal at my all-girls Catholic high school challenging the appropriateness of a particular punishment, my mother stood by my side. When the good Catholic nuns were all but ready to strangle me because I was "beating a dead horse," my mother simply encouraged them to respond to me in the same respectable and professional manner that I had addressed them.

My mother was - and still is - dedicated to everything that she does. I loved going into the office with her at Howard University and later the University of the District of Columbia. Even when I did not understand her role in admissions and recruitment, I knew that she was helping people. I knew that she treated each individual as if they were the only person in the world at the time. She did all she could and gave all she could to ensure every person had access to higher education. She assisted multitudes of people during her career. She coached, counseled, mentored and mothered many who had the opportunity to spend quality time with her. Because of her service, I knew I was called to serve.

One of the most influential times of my childhood was the summer when my mother was between jobs. During the day, she kept my sister, her brother (who is between my sister and I in age), a family friend who was like our little sister, and I. But my mother was dedicated to our education and exposure in the world. We had weekly trips to the library, museums and parks. Our days included school lessons in reading, writing and arithmetic. We had time for recreation and time for chores. My mother even put on her shorts and tennis shoes to run behind me as she taught me how to ride my bike. But more than that, I learned what it meant to make every moment of every day count. I learned how to balance work and fun. I learned that work can be fun and fun can work when you simply put all your heart into it. After a full day of running with us, my mother headed into her part-time evening job at the local Sears. My mother taught me that family is a priority and one must do whatever is required to support the family.

My mother also introduced me to God, church and service. In her example, I learned how these things are independent but related. My mother is a praying woman. Her relationship and reliance on God was demonstrated in her constant conversations with Him. There were even occasions when my mother was teased about her prayers. Although I know that did not feel good to her, she never stopped praying, nor did she stop encouraging her children to pray. I can truly say that my prayers are answered now partly because I learned to pray like my mother.

My mother was also very active in the church. She was on the different boards and organizations. She sang in the choir and served on the usher board. Her humble spirit does not always allow her to see her effectiveness and influence. But others can see, even in the way she is loved by the leadership and the congregation.

Since my mother was involved in church, so were her children. And my mother was not a 'drop them off' type of mom, so if we were in it, she was in it. She advised, chaperoned, hosted and chauffeured for every activity that my sister and I enjoyed. Those, and many other things, were her demonstration of service. And whether she knew or not, I was watching. Because of her presence and support, I stepped into youth leadership and service. This is where I learned to speak in public, pray in public, host a bake sale, organize a fashion show, run a meeting using Robert's Rules of Order, and a myriad of other things that would later come together in my personal and professional identity.

I remember reading the Scripture to my mother so I would be prepared when I got on the pulpit. I remember rehearsing my lines for the church or school play. Even if I insisted that I knew what I was doing, she made me do it anyway. Everything I did, I did because I saw my mother do it, and the things she did not do, she learned with me or from me. My mother taught me that being a perpetual student of life was not only fun, but also a necessary element for success.

For much of my upbringing, my mother was a student in college. She left college originally when she began her family. As my sister and I got older, she re-enrolled to complete her bachelor's degree in business. It took her a number of years and even more dedication. Since she would not make a big deal of it herself, we had to plan a surprise graduation ceremony for her. But seeing her walk across the back yard in full cap and gown was one of the proudest moments for our entire family. Because of her, I never questioned whether I would go to college or whether I would succeed. I knew if she did it, I wanted to do it.

My mother would always remind me to "dress for where you want to be, not for where you are." This was her way of encouraging me to walk in my vision even before I could fully see it. Since I wore a uniform to school and spend the rest of my time in church, this was not hard to do. As a matter of fact, when I got to college, I was once described as the girl who always dressed up. Even today, I have to remind myself to buy jeans and casual clothes. I am still most comfortable dressing up. Now I simply have a clearer vision of where up is.

I've had occasion to mentor and be mentored in my lifetime. I am grateful in advance knowing that many more opportunities will come my way. I know I am well prepared because Phyllis H. Lee would not have it any other way. And those who have come to mentor me in adulthood have followed her excellent example.

One esteemed follower is the author of this book, Barbara A. Perkins. I have confessed to Barbara that I did not like her upon our first meeting. It was not a personal assessment. But even then, she was pushing me into a great opportunity that was beyond my sight and belief at the time. So I made it about her and decided not to like her. But as God would have it, our paths had to cross again and I'm so blessed for it.

Barbara has been coach, sister, mother and friend, sometimes all in the same day. She has continued to push, pull, champion and cheer for me as I find my rightful place to stand.

In my opportunities to mentor, I strive to be all of the things I have learned from my mentors. I am human and perfectly imperfect. I am authentic and available. I teach those who want to learn and I learn from those I teach. I get my instruction from God and follow the guidance I am given. If and when I don't, I accept the necessary correction and get back in line. I love well and often. My mentors taught me these things and I pray someone will learn some measure of this from me.

My mother is aware that I have mentors in my life. Based on my conversations, she would identify Barbara as one of them. She could even identify many of the others I have been blessed to encounter. However, I do not believe she realizes she was the first mentor I ever had. I am not sure she knows the influence that she had and has in my life. She may not be clear that I wanted to be everything she was and do everything she did, and I am confident she does not know that of all the mentors I've had, she was and remains the best.

As a grown woman, I now know that the sun does not rise and set on my mother. However, I am a minister, teacher, counselor and coach today because of the faith in God she not only has, but also freely shared with me. What I know for sure is that when the sun rises and sets, God smiles because He knows at least one of the rays falls upon His daughter, Phyllis H. Lee. She is the daughter in whom He is well pleased. She is the mentor and mother to whom I am eternally grateful.

I love you mommy, Deborah 'ChinazaLungile' Lee!

Bridget Marie Nelson
Political Field Deputy
YOU ARE NEVER TOO OLD
FOR MENTORING

My story begins as an in-between child with more than three generations apart, my father was 18 years my mother's senior. My childhood was great. I had everything a little girl's heart desired, the dolls, the clothes and the love. My mentoring did not really begin until the death of my mother at the age of 54 when I was only 19. My father died the year before.

Although my mother herself was one of my greatest mentors ever, I would watch how all the neighbors would come to our house often to seek her advice on certain situations. So mentoring is really a part of my soul.

Growing up in a mostly black neighborhood was not so easy; a light-skinned, skinny girl with long hair and hazel eyes was not the norm in the 70's. I quickly became a target for bullying because of my looks. This resulted in me having low self-esteem. This is where my first mentor, other than my mother, came into being. Her name was Verdasten Williams; she was from the South and lived right across the street from us. I remember her house clearly. It was dark blue and was considered one of the ugliest houses on the block. No one would ever go visit Ms. Verdasten; they said she was a mean old lady who lived alone. They often called her the witch of the neighborhood. Ms. Verdasten was very nice to me and I had no problem with her at all. She talked to me about how she grew up in the south.

One day I was at her house and she asked me, "Why don't you enter into the homecoming court for your junior high school?" I quickly told her, "I could never do that." She asked, "Why?" I said,

"Because, look at me, I'm skinny and my legs are too skinny for that." Ms. Williams took me to the mirror and told me to look at myself real good in the mirror. She told me I had the perfect leg size and that I could be a leg model one day. That advice of looking at myself real good, remained with me throughout my life. It's not what others think of you, it is what you think of yourself that really matters.

Another mentor for me was Ms. Sandy, the mother of one of my best friends. She taught me family values. Ms. Sandy would also include me in everything her family did socially. She made me feel special in a way that really mattered. My mother had died and most of my extended family lived on the east coast. It was good for me and my son to be part of a family setting. We missed this dearly.

Ironically, as I became closer to Ms. Sandy's family, we discovered that she and my mother had worked for the same school board of education and in fact my mother had trained Ms. Sandy when she first began her job. This fact caused our relationship to grow even deeper.

Writing this essay has allowed me to reflect on how many wonderful people sowed into my life. Mrs. Felicia Johnson taught me the importance of education. She had three Master's degrees, which show you how much she believed in education. She would joke that if her dog could go to school and get a degree, she would send him.

I lived with Mrs. Johnson for some time. She was from Tulsa, Oklahoma, and enjoyed a successful marriage until her husband died. All of her children are college graduates from Howard University. She paid for their education and would tell me that she felt it was her responsibility to provide them with an education.

Mrs. Johnson would always ask me, "Do you know who you are?" That was a critical question for me, because I had forgotten who I was. She would talk to me about all of the basic life issues, making things so clear to me that her voice often guides me still today.

Each of the ladies I wrote about to this point, have all passed on; however, they will never be forgotten by me.

Lois Buckman, my current mentor, came into my life in recent years. We met as we were both working on a political fundraising team for a local politician. Through our day-to-day work, we began a relationship. Lois began to help me in ways that have added to my life positively. She is the most levelheaded and fair person I know. Her willingness to help others, no matter what the circumstances, is exemplary.

It was obvious to Lois that I needed someone to help me make better decisions. I needed to learn to listen to soften my heart just a little bit more. There were so many experiences that caused me pain that I began to be a bit mean-spirited and hard. Lois could see through me and my true self. Her actions towards me were kind and gentle. It made me reach for the best of me and begin to change.

Today, Lois is my mentor and godmother. She is the always-present shoulder I have to lean on. At the same time, she has come to know me well enough to know when to be firm with me and not let me forget who I am intended by God to be. There have been times when I was very angry about her advice to me, but once I calmed down, each time that happened, I realized it was for my good.

Mentoring has been the most important growth I took in my life. None of these women could replace what I had with my mother. However, I believe that my mother's spirit was present in each of these relationships.

When asked to do this essay, it brought such joy to my heart. I am happy to share how these ladies have helped me through difficult times in my life. I try to give back as much as I can through various organizations and non-profits. I want to give to someone else what these beautiful women have given to me.

Mentoring means you have an invested interest in someone and you only want the best outcome for them.

Barbara Perkins is such a blessing to women across the world, and I'm so honored to be a part of this journey with her.

I met Barbara through mutual friends and had many opportunities to speak with her at Lois's home, and later found out that

Barbara and her husband Stanley are long-time friends of my oldest brother Harry.

Melrita Evans Fortson
Founder: Los Angeles African American Women's
Public Policy Institute
Taking Charge of Your Life

The mentor who had the most impact on my life was my mother, Clara Evans Riley. With only an eighth grade education, she was very educated. Mom read everything and could discuss almost any subject matter. She even read the classifieds of the newspapers. When I questioned why she read them, she responded, "You never know what you may learn." Mom shared her unique expertise without recreating her image, but giving me the opportunity to create myself. The oldest of five, I was born and raised in the deep, segregated south. I knew black folks were treated differently, but as a young child, I did not understand why. Of course I learned. Mom taught us to stand tall, walk straight, look into the eyes, not the feet of the person you are speaking with, be respectful, value others' opinions, read the "good book," and believe in yourself. She emphasized sharing with others. Mom said our lives would take many interesting paths; therefore, we had to learn from them, and share with others. I called it teaching me values, but little did I know she was mentoring me.

My father died when I was only four years old. Mom remarried, and my stepfather died two weeks before my high school graduation. As the oldest, I had the responsibility to make sure all assigned chores were performed by my siblings. They resented taking my orders, and reminded me I was not mom. I reminded them of the consequences when mom returned home. Needless to say, they completed their tasks. When needed, I inserted subtle intimidation while applying the skills taught by my mom. Mentoring my siblings taught me to develop my nurturing skills, and assisted me in preparing for motherhood. I learned to be a role model for my siblings, and later for my daughter. Little did I know that I was developing the leadership skills that would dictate the path of my career. Mom said it was important to "speak right" so the words ain't, naw, huh, etc. were unacceptable in her presence. We used them with our friends, behind her back! Mom believed proper English would prepare us for the future and aid us with employment, despite living in the segregated south.

Mom also nurtured neighboring children who sought out her advice. We didn't think much of it because she was such a giver, whether it was food, clothes or advice. We just said, "That's the way mom is." I later learned, many of the parents did not teach or did not know how to teach their children the values our mom had provided. Those parents had no problems with our mom nurturing their children. Later in life, many of our childhood friends told our mom how much they loved her for the positive contributions she had made to their lives. Yes, mom practiced what she preached – sharing.

The definition of mentoring is very broad in words with the same end results. Simply put, John C. Crosby said, "Mentoring is a brain to pick, an ear to listen and a push in the right direction." According to Mike Turner, "The purpose of mentoring is always to help the mentee to change something – to improve their performance, to develop their leadership qualities, to develop their partnership skills, to realize their vision, or whatever. This movement is from where they are to where they want to be."

Per Oprah Winfrey, "A mentor is someone who allows you to see hope inside yourself." Suzanne Faure said, "Mentoring is a supportive learning process between a caring individual who shares knowledge, experience and wisdom with another individual who is ready and willing to benefit from this exchange to enrich their professional journey." In David Clutterbuck's opinion, "A mentor is a more experienced individual willing to share knowledge with someone less experienced in a relation of mutual trust." In my opinion, mentoring is a very powerful personal development and empowerment tool, providing an effective direction to help others to progress in their careers, as well as their personal lives.

I joined corporate America in the 1960s when the "glass ceiling" limited women's upward mobility. Promotional opportunities for women of color were even more limited. I was unaware of mentors until I read a magazine article. With this new knowledge, I set out to identify a mentor. I was a bargaining-unit employee interested in being promoted to a supervisory position. When I approached a potential, she told me she could not prepare me for promotional opportunities nor advise me. She stressed that I had to prepare myself just as she had done. Following that conversation, I felt insulted and belittled. I left that meeting believing I had made the biggest mistake of my future career. This experience made me reluctant to approach another potential mentor. I convinced myself I could learn what I needed to do to make myself a viable candidate for promotion.

Because I was not privy to a mentor, I concluded I could self-mentor/self-train. Since the Internet was not available like today, I set out to research the responsibilities of mentors. I surrounded myself with incredibly smart people and listened to them. I learned mentoring was not giving general advice; it was providing the necessary tools, strategies and techniques needed to achieve your goals. I had to learn what I was good at, and work hard to improve those skills. I also had to learn how to promote myself. I was the product, so I learned to market and sell my experiences, job skills, and interpersonal skills.

As the old cliché goes, when you cannot use *who* you know, you use *what* you know. At that time, it was company practice to allow employees to get on-the-job experience by submitting requests to be loaned to a department for vacation relief; I took advantage of this opportunity. I not only learned the skills of other positions, but gained recognition in those departments.

When I wanted to be promoted, I learned as much as possible about the potential job, talked to employees, when possible I met with the department manager, provided a copy of my resume, and asked to have my job skills compared to their department's needs. Once I discovered a position I wanted to be considered for, if necessary, I would visit the company or public library or take a college course. I wanted to prepare myself to be a top candidate. Wow, I sure could have benefitted from the Internet.

My success was contributed to by hard work, support, and good luck, but also through my achieved experiences. I learned to believe in myself. To further promote myself, I performed tasks I did not want to do, but I developed a reputation as a person who willingly accepted job assignments. Internal and external networking was a must. To increase my internal image, I invited the company's executives, from my immediate boss to the president, to attend external events, and introduced them to community, corporate, and other leaders whom they had not met – which made me look well connected.

Eventually I did not have to seek job opportunities, the department heads would seek me out. I learned to keep an updated resume. Following each promotion, one of my first tasks was to update my resume so I could be prepared should another job opportunity surface. Changes in the corporate atmosphere worked to my benefit; I started my career in an entry-level position and retired as a corporate executive.

No doubt mentoring should start at home, but that does not hold true for all children. Sadly, some parents do not know how to mentor their children or teach them values. Perhaps it was because they were never taught. Unfortunately, too many children grow up with no guidance and/or they learn from other children or their environment.

I was a member of my company's Youth Motivation Program with primary focus on inter-city schools. The intent was to encourage the kids to stay in school; go to and/or graduate from high school, and either go to college or learn a trade. At one middle school, I was assigned to an eighth grade class. After the introductions, I started my presentation by asking the students to think about what they wanted to do in the future, and we would discuss it later. At discussion time, one young boy told me he wanted to be a pimp and a drug king. I am sure he, as well as the other students, was expecting a shock reaction from me, but I was very calm. I informed him he was in charge of his future, and if that was his career choice, he still needed an education. I challenged his math skills, and reminded him that he needed to be educated before he could be a successful businessman. I informed him he should also take business and accounting courses. He told me he was expecting another lecture. I said it was not my desire to destroy his dreams, despite not agreeing with his career choices. My goal was to stress the importance of an education, and I hoped he not only understood the need, but also would incorporate it in his plan. The young man asked for my business card, and I gave it to him. Over the years he called me a few times. I received an announcement of his high school graduation, and he called to let me know he had been accepted at Howard University with a partial scholarship. He also wanted me to know he had changed his career goals because he had chosen not to be like the other guys in his neighborhood. My unrealistic goal was to reach all of those children, but I knew I had succeeded because I had reached one.

When addressing high school students, it is effective to incorporate goals with the lecture. It is important to let them know, while on this new journey, they will be faced with many challenges, successes, and failures in school, their career, and their personal life. Through it all, they must never view themselves as a victim, only a survivor.

Teach them to:
- Be motivated by their achievements, not their failures.
- Never make the mistake of resenting or measuring their success/failure against that of others. Instead, measure their success against the goals they have set for themselves.
- If you have to alter your goals due to circumstances beyond your control, do so with new vigor. My dad died two weeks before my high school graduation. Knowing my mom could not finance college without dad's income, I enlisted

in the U.S. Navy. From the Veterans' Benefits and my employer's tuition program, I acquired three degrees.

- As you grow, you have to continue to re-evaluate yourself, your goals, and your life.

Through the Youth Motivation Program, we provided classroom mentoring and, if requested, one-on-one mentoring. As a mother, I learned to evaluate the situation and listen to what was said before taking action, jumping to conclusions, or providing advice. In mentoring students, I also learned to assess their backgrounds and learn about their interests. Following such a discussion, together we prepared a plan for the next session including suggested reading. On career days, I would invite one of my adopted classes to tour my work location and have lunch with my staff. Because I sponsored events with several community-based organizations, I invited students to attend with their parents. It opened their eyes, and exposed them to a whole new world. When I was not available, I assigned one of my staff members to either meet with, or provide them with assistance. The students reacted very positively just knowing others cared. In return they strived to give their best.

Coaching and mentoring are both processes that enable individuals, businesses, and corporate clients to achieve their full potential. Coaching and mentoring share many similarities regardless of whether the services are offered in a paid or volunteer capacity. There are several levels of coaching and mentoring:

Personal/Individuals >>Business >>Executives
>>Performance >>Skills

There is an increasing trend for individuals to no longer rely on their employers to provide them with their career needs. Instead, many have taken greater responsibility for their professional development. Because the roles of jobs are changing at an increasing rate, skills coaches have to be highly experienced and competent in performing the skills they teach. The skills training should focus on the required skills of the job function. Business and executive coaching and mentoring are also on the increase. These changes create a need for qualified coaches and mentors.

- The coaches/mentors typically have a track record in the profession or have held executive roles
- Some coaches have worked in the profession or with high profile business leaders
- Some coaches have worked at board or CEO levels within high profile organizations
- Coaches use questioning techniques to facilitate their client's own thought process
- Coaches/mentors encourage a commitment to action
- They assist with the development of lasting personal growth and change
- Coaching and mentoring have proven to be highly successful intervention methods

Coaching and mentoring both focus on the individual. However, coaching is a process that enables learning and development. A successful coach is required to have knowledge and understanding of the process, as well as possess a variety of styles, skills and techniques that are appropriate to the coaching. Generally, the coach is not required to have direct experience of their client's formal occupation, except with skills and performance coaching. Mentoring enables an individual to follow in the path of an experienced and wiser person who can pass on knowledge and experiences, and make transitions in their way of thinking.

The coach/mentor must observe, listen and ask questions to understand the individual's situation. We have to work within the area of the individual's personal competence. We have to be supportive and non-judgmental of the individuals, their views, lifestyle and aspirations. A coach or mentor ensures that the individual develops personal competencies, and not allow them to develop unhealthy dependencies on the coach or mentor. Supporting the individual in setting realistic goals and establishing methods of assessing their progress is a must. A good coach will manage the relationship to make sure the client receives the appropriate level of services. As a coach or mentor, share concepts to assist in the development of your clients. Transitioning from dependent to independent, many well-known goals include, but are not limited to:

- Identify someone, internally, whom you believe has the ability to open doors for you and recommend you for promotional opportunities
- Learn that it's okay to fail as long as you accept your failures as growth experiences, and not deterrents of growth.
- Be willing to take calculated risks. Risk-taking is part of succeeding.
- Strengthen your self-confidence by learning to build on your attributes. Discover what you are good at and make every effort to be better.
- Criticism often follows success. Do not be afraid of being criticized. You have heard the expression "constructive criticism" is good. That's bull; there is nothing constructive about criticism, but it goes with the job. You can actually learn from criticism.
- Pave your own road. Ralph Waldo Emerson said, "Don't go where the path may lead you, instead go where there is no path and you leave the trail for others to follow".

Mentoring should be taken seriously because it does change lives, it refine theirs. Through mentoring, people are taught *how* to think, not *what* to think. Peter Drucker said, "No one learns as much about a subject as one who is forced to teach it." Mentoring is a growth opportunity for the mentor, as well as the mentee. Mentees should be challenged to think for themselves, and find their own voices.

You have succeeded as a mentor or coach if the individuals take the tools you have provided to develop their leadership skills, as well as, realize their vision. Anne Frank said, "Everyone has inside himself a piece of good news! The good news is that you really don't know how great you can be, how much you can love, what you can accomplish and what your potential is."

Corina Mena-Aikhionbare
Real Estate Developer
A Solid Foundation

I lived in a town of a thousand people, founded by my father, until I was sixteen years old. If this sounds small to you, you are absolutely correct. The town was small, but filled with amazing people who traveled and brought back exciting books, magazines and toys that created a window to the world outside of my little world. I was surrounded by amazing women and men who shared their knowledge, guidance, love and kindness. It started with parents who loved each other so much and strived to let their eight children know it. Mommy and daddy were a special team.

One look from mommy, the disciplinarian, and you knew it was time to change whatever you were doing. She demanded that we all ate together at a table set for a king or queen. No one cooked like her. The smell of homemade bread would wake us up in the mornings. Daddy was kind and gentle with my sister and me. He promised the boys that if they hit their sisters they would be sorry. That was all he needed to say about that and all five brothers understood. Daddy never embarrassed us. If he received a complaint about us from anyone, he would ask for an explanation in the most encouraging voice and without judgment. He was fair and he trusted us to do as we were taught always. None of us wanted to disappoint our parents, so we did.

My Granny Mena loved her grandchildren more than life. We often gathered under the mango tree in her front yard to listen to her fairytales. She was the best at storytelling. We did not miss the fact that we did not have a television. The stories were always about how good behavior, manners and kindness would overcome anything. One story that I remember so well was about the girl who was so kind and good that her arm grew back after being cut-off by her very bad brother. I also remember the story about the man who studied so hard that he outsmarted and captured a group of bad monkeys.

Then there was the story about the children who lost both parents, but found magical melon seeds that provided for all their needs. Clearly, the moral of her stories was always the same; this was how she taught us without making us feel like we were in a classroom.

Granny Mena demanded proper behavior. We had to sit properly at the dinner table, maintain perfect posture, and say "please" and "thank" you all the time. We could not say "good morning" to everyone as a group, we had to greet *each* person by name. But the most profound thing about Granny Mena was that she was consistent. We were all treated equally, and the rules were not bent. She did not hit or yell, but instead she would send you to sit alone in a quiet place or if the deed was really naughty, then you would kneel for a few minutes while facing a wall. All of these things were symbols of love. We knew that she loved us and she was preparing us for our adult lives. This was my first mentor.

Next was my amazing aunt Louise, she could whip up food in minutes to feed the entire neighborhood. She had seven children and more godchildren than anyone I knew. All of the children loved being in her home. She did it all it seemed. She made my very first maxi-dress, because I really wanted one. She gave me the money to go buy the fabric and made the dress in less than an hour, it seemed like there was nothing she could not do.

I was her favorite, or so she made me feel. I am sure my sisters and brothers would say the exact same thing. She made us all feel that special. She was strict, but sweet. This was her lesson, she made you feel like there was no one else more important than you, but you had to follow the rules. She was and still is my favorite, from her I learned to share, give without hesitation, and love unconditionally.

My godmother Zab, she seemed ten feet tall, but in actuality was about 5'10. She was elegant, perfect smile, posture, educated, smart, selfless, and carried my village on her shoulders. My dad called her daughter, and she loved him like a dad. They planned my life. Together they made sure I got all the best my little village had to offer and more. Being with her was always so easy for me, because she was always so truthful. However, she also kept the inappropriate away from me and would let me know when topics were off limits for me.

My daddy passed in 1986 and she assumed the role of family guardian. She mentored most of the people in my village, from the teachers, to the elders who lacked her sophistication and experience. She continues to teach by example. She remains the person who motivates me and encourages me to push past any barriers.

Today, I spend much of my time giving to my nieces and nephews words of encouragement and advice as I have been given by so many. I have become the mentor to them that my aunts and others were to me. I have spent my life creating a home where my children and friends will know, it is the place to come to; whether it is to attend a study group or get a home-cooked meal, learn manners, find love and patience or have good old fashion fun without television.

For them, I wish to be as the elders were for me. My message to them is family is important and home is where you get your encouragement. Family will always be available when needed. I expect them to take, but also expect them to give back.

Children truly emulate the adults in their lives. The people, peers and family who reach out to us and depend on us to give the best of who we are all the time, so choose wisely.

I am appreciative of the invitation by my friend Barbara Perkins to share a bit of my story, with the hope that it would inspire in some meaningful way. Barbara and I met a few years ago and found that we share love and laughter for many of the same things. Our relationship continues to grow as she pushes me. I push back and together we thrive to be better people.

Maxine Attong
Gestalt Organizational Development Practitioner
& Writer
FOR A LIFETIME

For the last twenty years I have had the same mentor. We have never had a formal relationship, in which we were introduced as mentee and mentor, but now that I understand the nature of these roles I can comfortably call our relationship that.

I had recently qualified as a Certified Management Accountant and had a great interest in Activity Based Costing (ABC). I was responsible for developing a pilot program at work that would cost the products that we generated at the office. I had read a few books on the topic and had some of my own ideas that I wanted to discuss with someone, hence the reason that a mutual colleague introduced me to Jack.

Jack was the Chief Financial Officer at a multi-national manufacturing plant that churned out a number of products. At the plant, Jack had just introduced an Activity Based Costing program and could give me good insights on how this worked. I was excited to talk to him and hear what he had to say and hopefully learn a thing or two.

I first met Jack on a Saturday afternoon. I drove for about an hour to get to the plant, and was ushered to his office by a security guard. As he got up to meet me I noticed there was an ashtray on his desk and a cigarette in his left hand. He firmly held my right hand with his and introduced himself. I in turn did the same.

I sat, and slowly we started talking. I was never uncomfortable, it seemed like the most natural thing in the world to be sitting opposite a man whom I had never met and watch him smoke cigarette after cigarette. We spoke about Activity Based Costing and how it worked, some of the pitfalls of implementation and I shared my ideas with him.

When our chat ended and I returned to the parking lot, I was shocked that it was dark outside. I spent over four hours chatting with a total stranger, and yet there seemed to be nothing strange about that, because I knew that I would be back to chat some more. I had found someone who spoke my language, who knew what I meant, someone who listened to me and someone who willingly shared their knowledge and experience and someone from whom I could learn a lot.

We met many times at his office over my accounting career. Always on a Saturday, I would drive to his office and have a chat, leaving when the sun was fleeing the sky. Over the years, I told him about my ambitions and what I wanted to do, I shared my frustrations around office politics and we celebrated my successes and extracted lessons from my failures. From my meetings with him I learned to not take myself too seriously. I found someone who celebrated my risk-taking nature even though he himself worked at the same company for many years.

When I decided to move on from that job, I went to him to discuss the idea. I was not looking for advice about *whether* I should leave; I was looking for confirmation that I *should* leave. Instead, he helped me explore the reasons why I was leaving and what I was hoping to gain at my job. I would return to him to have these types of discussions around my career choices.

When I worked as a consultant and was frustrated by my clients, Jack helped me to identify the pattern in my behavior that triggered these frustrations.

He never took my side, he was always rational and pushed me to think, to look at my role in every situation and to take responsibility and accept culpability when necessary. Though those were difficult and uncomfortable situations, I never felt reprimanded. I always walked away with my dignity intact, even though I may have been feeling like crap.

His office was a no-bullshit zone that required me to tell the absolute truth about everything. He heard every word that I said and everything I said mattered. In that room my voice was important, my opinion counted and I felt that he had a genuine interest in me and my world.

He talked, I listened, I talked and he listened. Then he would ask me questions.

He was a curious man and for whatever reason he was interested in me and my career.

His was an open invitation on any given Saturday, if I had an idea, something that I wanted to put into words, I knew that there was someone willing to hold the space for me to discuss and decide. There was only one unstated rule, "No crap." I knew that I would be called on it, and that I needed to check my intentions and to explain without rationalizing my thoughts and behavior.

When my world changed, I lost contact with him since I no longer wanted to be an accountant.

After a period of many years in 2010, I reached out to him to share my new venture - I wanted to write books. He is one of the most voracious readers that I have ever met, so I thought he would be the perfect person to pitch my book to. By then he was retired and I visited him at his home.

It was he who told me that the draft chapters of my book, Change or Die, was missing the essence of who I am and that I needed to think about what I wanted to give the audience. He encouraged me to put my experiences and the real life examples that I worked on into the text.

It was to him that I turned to discuss the safe space concept, which is the foundation of my second book – "Lead Your Team To Win." As the book grew, Jack was the first person to read the chapters, give feedback, ask questions and to make his comments. It was exciting for me to share this experience with him and to be back in a relationship that involved him asking me powerful questions that pushed my performance levels.

Even as I wrote, I noticed that I was not relying on him as I did before, but I was sharing my world with him and he willingly accepted the invitation. I still call when I have great news and opportunities, but I don't need his validation. Today I feel that I have a deep and true relationship with Jack that has matured into a friendship that takes place in the cocoon of his home. I have never thought of him as a father figure, a potential lover or as someone I needed to prove myself to. I have always thought of him as Jack forever in my corner and someone who I could bounce ideas off of.

If I could change one thing about our relationship, I would have wished that I had the courage to tell Jack about my personal struggles. He never said that we could not talk about my personal life or asked me to keep it strictly professional, but because he never explicitly invited me to talk about my personal life, I never brought it up. In retrospect, I could have gone with some introspection around that as well.

At work, I mentor two young men who are identified as future executives. It is a wonderful opportunity to support them in their careers and ambitions. I mirror my mentorship, on the beautiful relationship that I am lucky to still share with Jack. I ensure that with my mentees I do the following ten things each and every time that we meet.

1) I create a safe space for them to enter and confide in me.

2) I present myself as someone who they can trust and retain this trust by being confidential.

3) I listen to them and ask them questions to bring them to awareness.

4) I do not judge whatever they are saying.

5) I ask, "What is your role in the story you shared?"

6) I do not take responsibility for the interaction. They call me, and I am available.

7) I ensure that they feel seen and heard at the meetings.

8) I am genuinely interested in their growth and development.

9) I am open to long-term relationships with them. They can come and go as the please.

10) I explicitly give them permission to discuss personal or work issues when we meet.

Rhonda Sams
Entrepreneur, Community Events Organizer
MENTORING, A PROCESS
AND A JOURNEY

In so many ways I am like the element air. One of my earliest memories of my childhood was when my aunt Erma, or Auntie as we so lovingly called her, compared me to the likes of a butterfly. Auntie Erma was the youngest of my mom's sisters and was always encouraging me to spread my wings and fly. She loved birds and was an avid collector of all types of images of birds. Auntie Erma was also feisty, uninhibited, and fun. She was a top executive at her firm and had the same heart and drive for family. She never had any children of her own, so I was spoiled by her love and attention. As a tall and skinny kid, I felt awkward growing up, but my auntie Erma always assured me of my beauty.

One of her gifts to me was the book, Jonathan Livingston Seagull by Richard Bach. It was my favorite childhood book and in many ways it was a foreshadow for my life. My Auntie Erma was one of my very first mentors. She taught me self-acceptance, joy and freedom.

I am an entrepreneur, community events organizer, and spiritual seeker. My greatest joy comes from creating events where people can share stories, embrace support, and/or give support to others.

As a teenager, I looked for examples of people who were living the life I wanted to create for myself. From the African American business owner to the motivational speaker, author, minister, I craved their knowledge, and I wanted to know their stories. Much of my teenage encounters, however, were through reading or listening to them speak in public forums like my church. I was fortunate to have grown up in Chicago during the 80's, in what I deem the Renaissance Revival. There was a tapestry of rich examples of creativity all around me on the south side of Chicago. This tapestry, although more passive in witnessing as an experience, still helped to shape in my sub-conscious mind that dreams were possible. The mentor of my teenage years was the Rev. Dr. Johnnie Coleman, the founder of Christ Universal Temple.

My parents were extremely forward thinking when it came to religion. Their parents raised them to respect and fear the Lord, having been raised Pentecostal (mom) and Catholic (dad). As adults, my parents longed for a new approach to religion, and so they exposed my brother and me to New Thought teachings from Christ Universal Temple (CUT). I remember when I first met Rev. Johnnie. It always amazed me that she allowed us to call her by her first name.

Rev. Johnnie was a towering black woman with such determination and power. I felt like I could grow up to be like her, walking with my head tall and having something truly empowering to share with others. I never grew weary of listening to her sermons on the power of our thoughts and actions. She showed me the power of clarity, prayer, and manifestation. I was one of her babies, as she lovingly called the children who grew up in her Youth Expressing Christ (YEC) program. Even when I moved away from CUT to visit other churches, I will never forget the impact that Rev. Johnnie Colemon had on my life. It was at CUT that I witnessed her openness to other faith communities, and her example would play a huge part in my adult growth and development.

College offered me the gift of mentorship through my advisor, Robert Hill, of Syracuse University. He encouraged me to start a local newspaper on campus, and he would advise me throughout my college career. Robert Hill gave me my first campus job in alumni relations, and included me in many of the campus meetings on donor fundraising. The mentoring experience continued after college as well. Robert Hill helped me land my first job!

After graduating from college, my career blossomed, but the bug for entrepreneurship kept calling me. As a third generation entrepreneur, I knew what I wanted to do, but didn't know how to make it profitable. I wanted to support others with empowering events and forums. In 2002, I founded the Sistah Summit Retreat and had the privilege of meeting many of the "Black Pearls" that Barbara speaks about in this book. It was here that I also met Barbara Perkins. I remember witnessing the beautiful bond of friendship and sisterhood that she shared with several of the speakers during our women's retreat. I wanted this as well. All of the speakers of the women's retreat served as mentors for me. They inspired me and taught me how to "pass it forward" to others. When I look back over my life, one of the greatest joys I experienced came from building the Women's Retreat. It is true that your greatest gift as a mentor/teacher is the very thing you are here to learn yourself. For me, relationships are one of the key channels of my life's design and purpose.

Right now I am a mentor for the young people in my family. I am also a mentor for women that I'm building support groups around for infertility. I'm the type of mentor who wants to work beside my mentees. I think that's the best way I can serve as mentor. I do that in my career as an event producer and through my social and civic duties with public service organizations.

The most important message that I want to leave you with is this: You are already a mentor. The question is how much intentionality and awareness you are willing to bring to this awesome opportunity that God has given us to serve. So many times we don't think we're ready to mentor, or putting the label on it makes it feel like "more of a responsibility" than we think we might be ready for. We are all still learning. So mentoring is organic and it's not a finite destination. It's a process and a journey. It's also a give and take.

We learn as much from the people we mentor as they learn from us. Ultimately, I think the greatest gift I've received and the one that I'd like to give is when "mentoring" becomes "witnessing" and an accountability partner. Celebrating their accomplishments and calling out what they may not see just yet. Mentoring keeps the tapestry of our community strong. We need it to thrive and to survive. At all stages we are either the teacher or the student. Mentoring allows us to experience both. I'm a builder. I see the need and want to fill it. There is no greater joy when we work with people of like-minds to build together. That's what mentoring offers us, a chance to build and share in, and participate in, a strong community. So let's get to building.

As a butterfly, I've come across many pearls/mentors, and they continue to encourage me to fly, and to take courage when I have to make course corrections, land to replenish and build, and when I have to accelerate to new heights. This is what I give as a mentor as well. I like to encourage others to take flight and manifest their true-life design.

Rustin Lewis, Ph.D.
Executive Director of a nonprofit organization
Don't Talk About It -
But Be About It!

I am a concerned American citizen. I am concerned that the many generations that follow will not be prepared academically, emotionally, socially or financially for the speedily changing world ahead. I am the son and brother of three social workers. I am a motivator for many young men and women who have crossed my path albeit via mentoring organizations or family friends. I am multi-dimensional with too many interests to name; however, my love for society and commitment to equality is unwavering.

I met Barbara Perkins along my journey to help others. At the time, she was Executive Director for the Los Angeles CARES Mentoring Movement. We connected because of our shared commitment and passion for mentoring the young, and uplifting underserved communities.

In retrospect, mentoring was a pivotal component for my growth and development. In September 2014, I spoke to a group of young professionals during the Congressional Black Caucus Foundation's Emerging Leaders luncheon. As I prepared my comments, I questioned the impetus that afforded me the opportunity to be here. My first thought was that I had great parents and grandparents.

As a child I can remember my grandfather saying to avoid fights and arguments, and both of my parents encouraging me to "Stay on the right side of right." Both of my parents pursued their education in the field of social work, and subsequently became administrators in their fields.

As a teenager, my parents encouraged my sister and I to work during our summer break with social service programs. For several summers I worked as a youth counselor with underserved children, and my sister worked in a food pantry. Our parents and grandparents often spoke of education and the importance of attaining as much education as possible. I can recall seeing framed diplomas and degrees in our basement and in my parent's office. Too young to understand the magnitude of their true purpose, I did understand that they were symbols of academic accomplishment and struggle. The foundation that my first mentors (my parents) put in place has sustained me throughout my life.

As I matriculated through college and graduate school, a number of people crossed my path who, in hindsight, were mentors. Mentoring is often viewed as a structured effort, but sometimes elders are unaware that they are mentoring their village. After I completed college, Dr. Obie Clayton offered me employment with the Morehouse Research Institute (MRI). During my employment with MRI, he became a role model and inspired me to pursue a doctorate. The issues that MRI researched were dear to my heart, and for the first time I discovered how to mold my passion for issues of inequality with my personal goal of obtaining a higher education. After working there for several years, Dr. Clayton encouraged me to pursue new opportunities and expand my work and education portfolio. His mentoring set a course for me to continue my education, and challenged me to leave my comfort zone.

Soon after, I found employment with the 100 Black Men of America. The 100 Black Men of America exposed me to a group of African American men who were well educated, in many cases financially established, and yet concerned about the future of boys of color. This organization, under the leadership of Thomas W. Dortch, Jr. and Dwayne Ashley, served over 10,000 youth annually, but I was the recipient of the internal mentoring that took place. I learned a lot of business practices and best practices for nonprofit management. My exposure to their leadership style fine-tuned my interests in being a community-leader, a businessman, and contributor to the future of our society. These are the people whom I credit with laying a strong foundation by which I have been able to fulfill my life's passions. Without these experiences and opportunities my career path and life may have been very different. Today, because of the shoulders on which I was allowed to stand, I am the Executive Director of a nonprofit organization that helps youth prepare for college and career opportunities. Because of those shoulders, I have completed my BA, Masters and Doctoral degrees.

For more than two decades I have preached to our youth two things that I know to be true:

1. Don't talk about it, but be about it!

I have learned that we are all guilty of talking about what we want to do in life. It does not matter whether or not you are talking about going to college, becoming a mentor or an anesthesiologist. The central point is do not spend your years talking about it with your family and friends. Start making a plan to get it done. There are many things that I've spent time talking about doing, and have yet to do. However, when I stopped talking about my desire to obtain a doctorate and began making moves, only then did it become a reality for me. And quite honestly, after taking the first step, it becomes a shorter journey.

2. Life is all about exposure and decisions.

The more that we open our minds to and let others expose us to positive, new experiences, the more likely we are to reach for higher planes. No matter how old you are, we must all challenge ourselves to try new things, albeit new neighborhoods to live in, new cities, new countries, new foods, and new friends. Our exposure informs our decisions. We all make decisions every single day. As I reflect upon my life, it was simply the decisions that I made that greatly impacted my life for better or for worse. And so, the magic of mentoring is that we should embrace the pearls of wisdom that we are exposed to, and make decisions to support our dreams based on what we have learned from our mentors.

Wendy Gladney Dean
Founder of Forgiving For Living, Inc.
A Lifetime of Mentoring

I've had the privilege of knowing Barbara Perkins for over a decade (and I'm sure much longer than that). She always reminds me of the definition of a mentor, one who is an experienced or trusted advisor. She has a unique way of sharing information, especially with sisters that make you feel stronger, wiser and taller. So when she shared with me about her new book project, "Magic of Mentoring: Pearls of Wisdom," and asked if I would be interested in submitting a piece, how could I pass up such an opportunity? This is one of those opportunities that come along in life where the gates are opened wide and you can walk through to share what God has given you, a unique voice to share.

Everything about the title of this new endeavor intrigues me. Mentoring has always been a part of my life, whether I understood it or not. I would have never put the word "magic" in the same title of mentoring, but when one thinks about what magic is, the power of apparently influencing the course of events, it definitely fits. I also feel that it is very important for us who've gone before to reach back and share pearls of wisdom we've gleaned along the way. Pearls represent a hard lustrous mass that had to go through a lot to come out as precious and refined as it does. As a member of the Alpha Kappa Alpha Sorority, since the beginning, pearls have been a symbol of our sisterhood. So again I feel honored to string together the knowledge and information I've learned through the years on the power of mentoring.

My childhood in many ways left a lot to be desired. I came from a broken home where my mother abandoned me as a little girl before I even reached school age. My father was one who ran the streets, and pretty much was caught up in a riotous lifestyle. I became a victim of his environment, being exposed to pool halls, gambling shacks, women of the night, and the lust of my father's eyes and hands. In my formative years I did not have the protection of my mother or the nurturing of her very being. However, I did fall into the hands, over time, of my paternal grandmother, aka, "Mother Dear," my aunt Dolores, and from time to time, stepmothers, women in the community, church and school. These were truly my first examples of how a mentor can affect your life.

There were plenty of women that came in and out of my life over the years, but few would I consider a role model or mentor. When I think about the role models or mentors that were in my life as I was growing up, I must start with my grandmother, known to most as Mother Dear. My grandmother was a very hard worker. She was the mother of nine children, a host of grandchildren, and even more great-grandchildren. Oftentimes she had to pick up the slack where her children fell short in raising their own children. I happened to be one of those who were often left in her care. What is it about grandmothers that make you feel safe and that life would get better? Although she really didn't know how or what to accept about what happened to me by my father, her son, she just kept a steady beat keeping all of us going. I can't really say that she ever just sat me down and said do this or don't do that; she truly lead by example. I listened to her every word and watched her every movement.

My grandmother believed in setting routines, and we had to follow them. She would make us get up early every morning, whether we had school, church or not. When we would ask if we could sleep in she would say, "Okay, you can sleep in until 6:30 a.m. (our normal getting up time was between 5:00 – 5:30 a.m.)." What's interesting is I still get up today between 5:00 – 5:30 a.m. She would always say, "The early bird gets the worm." I didn't understand that phrase back then, but as I've gotten older, I get it. She also taught us to always be polite, honor our elders, and to have manners. I came from very humble beginnings. We didn't have a lot, but what we had was clean and orderly. My grandmother made us attend church. We had to be card-carrying members of African American (back then known as Black or Negro) organizations such as the Urban League and the NAACP. She made us write 'thank you' notes (of course that was way before email and social media communication). She gave me tools that have taken me through life. These very same principles are what I taught to my children and to those I have the privilege of mentoring. They formed the core of my values.

The second person I would like to share with you is Sabra, my father's second wife. She's also the mother of my sisters, and the woman I named my daughter after. As a little girl I used to sit and admire her beauty and the way she dressed. She, too, played a very important role in my life and mentored me even when she didn't know that she was doing so. She was my first impression of family, where a mother cooked meals and made a house a home. Our family life together didn't last long, but it left an indelible impression on me as to the beauty of a home, the term happy holidays, and it was the only time my brother and sisters and I were all under the same roof together as a family. When I reflect back to this time in my life, what really makes all of this so interesting is my stepmother was just a child herself when she came into my life. She started as my babysitter and eventually became my mom.

Next there's Cheryle. She was truly a Southern Belle. She hailed originally from New Orleans, but somehow landed in Riverside, California. I was introduced to her by a friend who told me Cheryle was looking for someone to help her from time to time with babysitting for her two young sons, and possibly helping her around the house with light chores. I was now the babysitter, but I still longed for someone who would accept me as their daughter and love me unconditionally. For some reason I felt that since Cheryle had two sons and no daughters at the time, she would notice me. She was extremely kind to me, and I blossomed under her attention. She came into my life during a very crucial point when I really needed that feminine touch to help me transition from being a little girl to a young lady. She took time with me, she listened to me, she helped groom me, and she bought me clothes that took me from elementary school to junior high. She helped me understand the meaning of being a "lady." But again the fairytale only lasted for a short time.

During high school I had a teacher by the name of Yvonne Ashe. She added a whole new perspective with me as it relates to what it means to have a mentor. She was my math teacher, and although she was a bit tough on me, she really loved and cared for me. As I approached my senior year, she started asking me a lot of questions about my plans and goals as it related to college. To be honest with you, I really didn't have many. I knew I wanted to go, but I was confused about the process. Although I came from a family with members that attended college, no one actually sat down with me to really prepare me for that step in life. Again, my parents were absent.

My high school counselor recommended that I go to the local junior college, which at first sounded logical to me. When Ms. Ashe discovered that I was an honor student, head varsity cheerleader, President of the Black Student Union, active in the church and community, she said that junior college was not my option. While my high school counselor was a white male who didn't take interest in me or my future, Ms. Ashe was determined to make sure I had a chance for success. She made a commitment to me and she was determined to help me so that I wouldn't fall through the cracks. Because of her efforts and mentorship, I not only attended the University of California at Los Angeles, but I also was a recipient of an academic scholarship.

There's a saying that people come into our lives for a reason, season, or a lifetime. When I was a mother going through a divorce and trying to find my way, my children and I began going to a church called Mount Zion. While there, I met Mother Elma Jackson. Mother Jackson was my prayer partner, my confident, and my mentor at a time when I felt like I was drowning. She truly loved me unconditionally, and encouraged me every step of the way. She recently passed away, but her voice and her wisdom will stay with me for the rest of my life. She was an angel sent by God and encouraged me in such a way that it helped me be a better adult. We don't stop needing "mentors" just because we're grown.

There came a time in my life when I really needed to connect with my birth mother and her family. My mother and I had an opportunity to get to know one another, and I even took care of my mother for close to eleven years. However, when I met her twin sister, my Aunt Kathy, I felt like I was looking into a mirror. There were so many things about me and my mannerisms that were explained as soon as I met her and spent time with her in her home. Her presence in my life helped clarify things that others were not able to tap into. I believe we are all products of both nature and nurture in our lives. My aunt Kathy, now my momma Kathy filled a hole that no one else was able to fill.

As I opened this story, I shared that mentoring has been part of my life for as long as I can remember. Because of all of the things I've experienced and gone through, I've had many people open up and talk to me. One of the ways I formally structured helping others or mentoring is through the organization, Forgiving For Living, Inc. It was established in 1999 with the mission to help at-risk girls between the ages of 13-18 overcome behavior and mental health issues in addition to issues of low self-esteem due to depression, abuse, and or abandonment. We help provide the necessary tools to live a healthy life through an Ambassador Program, workshops, and an annual conference, which offers mentoring and life skills. To date, we've touched the lives of over 3,000 girls. The vision of the organization is to give girls hope and purpose through understanding the power and importance of forgiveness. We hope to restore their self-esteem, self-confidence, and provide tools for a better and more productive life.

Over the years I've formed the opinion that everyone should have a Paul, Timothy and Barnabas as learned from the Bible. Paul was a teacher (mentor), Timothy was a student (mentee) and Barnabas was an encourager.

We should all be a mentor, have a mentor, and encourage those in our life. If I could share or leave one pearl of wisdom with everyone who will read this book of knowledge, it would be to just be yourself and know that you're good enough, just as you are, to touch another person's life. I truly believe in the power of one, and for each one to reach one.

As I bring this piece to a close, I find it interesting how life will bring us full circle. An organization that I was introduced to many years ago, called Sisters at the Well, founded by Barbara Perkins, chose me as one of their honorees for their 2014 "We See You" Awards. Thank you, Barbara Perkins, for acknowledging the work I've done for years with mentoring the lives of young ladies between 13-18 years of age, as well as others. I truly believe it is incumbent upon all of us to reach back and pull someone up with us as we climb.

Vanessa Leon
Urban Planner
Identity, Triumph And Vision:
A Tribute to My Mentors

I was a confused little black girl and though I grew up in New York City, I did not have a lot of people to turn to in helping me make sense of my confusion. I was the first person in my family born in the United States; I struggled with making sense of the connections that I was forming in my mind in regards to race relations in this country. For me, the intersections between race and class primarily manifested itself throughout my educational pursuits and the more I excelled, the more I was made to feel like I did not belong, despite my achievements. This greatly perplexed me and I could not understand why. Furthermore, given that my academic performance enabled me to benefit from specialized schools and programs outside of my culturally diverse neighborhood, I also concluded that place mattered in terms of the opportunities available to people based on where they lived and the racial make-up of a particular locality, since there were less and less people that looked like me in these settings.

This conundrum followed me throughout my teenage years and ultimately reached a climax when I received several scholarships, totaling over $100,000, to attend a prestigious predominately white university in Massachusetts.

With the unwavering guidance of my first mentor, Dr. Ibrahim Sundiata of the History and African and African American Studies department, I finally began to understand the complex legacy that I had inherited as an African descendant, as well as my positioning in the world as an emerging black professional. Well before that however, I attended an elementary school in a fairly rough neighborhood of South Jamaica, Queens, for first and second grades. My family had just moved to Queens from Brooklyn and my parents' first choice options for my brother and I that were closer to home were already at capacity. I never felt safe in the surrounding area of my school and every morning, I made it a point to make a straight-line attempt off of my yellow school bus to the school entrance as quickly as possible.

I also recall the student body being almost entirely black and that the majority of us qualified for the city's less-than appetizing free or reduced lunch. There were two classmates who were fortunate enough to bring their neatly packed sandwiches, boxed juices and gummy fruit snacks every day and I was often disheartened to know that my mother had neither the time nor the means to send me with a loaded lunch box since she worked two to three jobs on average to support us. At the tender age of six therefore, I resolved that if education was my pathway out of poverty – a message that was constantly underscored in my immigrant household – I would work as hard as I could to ensure that one day I would be able to purchase all the fruit snacks I wanted just like those two little girls with the pink and purple lunch boxes.

When I got to the end of second grade, I and one other classmate (a Puerto Rican boy whose family was in the process of moving to Florida) earned the highest scores on the states standardized exam for our grade. The decision was made by the school administrators and my parents to transfer me to an Especially Gifted Children's (EGC) program in another section of Queens. My new school was in Cambria Heights, which happens to be the only neighborhood in the United States where the median income of the black population exceeds that of their white neighbors. There were two EGC classes per grade from third to fifth grade and my EGC cohort all throughout was much more racially diverse than the rest of the primarily black classes in the school. Third grade particularly stands out because I have vivid memories of learning about painters like Picasso and Leonardo, reading full-length chapter books, and having our weekly Daily News subscriptions so that we could monitor the New York Stock Exchange in the newspaper on 'Stock Tuesdays.' Ms. Sheila O'Neal's fifth grade was memorable as well because it was the first and last time I would learn about black history in an academic setting before encountering Dr. Sundiata almost a decade later in college. By the time I made it to Townsend Harris High School, a specialized school located on the Queens College campus, my graduating class of about 260 students had about fifteen to twenty black girls and two black boys. It always bothered me that the class right before us had no black boys.

Arriving at Brandeis University as the second in my family to attend college was truly an honor. My sister, Scherly, now a medical doctor, was the first and I was proud to embark on the path that she had blazed for herself and the rest of the family. In addition to receiving a full-tuition leadership scholarship valued at over $100,000 from the POSSE Foundation, I also received a needs-based scholarship from the Bill and Melinda Gates Foundation as well as several other scholarships of varying amounts to help pay for my books and other necessities. With these early accomplishments I was proud because I knew how hard I worked to earn every dime.

Despite Brandeis being a predominately Jewish institution and the reality that I was one of two black girls in my entire dormitory freshman year, I was thrilled to be there because the institution had a reputation for being a school of social justice. Little did I know that I was going to spend the next few years living the social justice that I thought I would be there to study. I certainly didn't know that I was embarking upon a life-altering journey when I selected my first-year university seminar (USEM) the summer before arriving on campus. Professor Sundiata's "United States and Africa" seminar, coupled with the racialized experiences that I began having as a Brandeis student, would profoundly shape how I engaged with the world around me, my perception of self and the mark I am continually making on the world.

Throughout the course, and in many ways throughout his work, Professor Sundiata was keen to identify the narratives that form around identity and the various ways that those narratives shaped the people and societies within which they formed. One such narrative that began emerging for me was that somehow, because of my identity as a black woman, I did not belong at Brandeis. During the first few weeks of my first semester, a white hall mate approach me as I was finishing my shower and blatantly remarked that she had seen and heard of black people but had never spoken to 'them' – that is until she met me. She went on to say that she did not "believe in all this diversity and multicultural crap and that the Jews should stay with the Jews, the Asians should stay with the Asians and that the blacks should stay with the blacks." She pointedly concluded by asking, "Why did you come to Brandeis anyway?"

As I grappled with the cycle of shock, anger, shame and bitterness from this experience with Yael Klein, I began to realize that somehow the storied histories of the African Diaspora that I was learning about in Professor Sundiata's course were somehow correlated with my daily reality as a black student on campus. It greatly pained me that I did not know how to make sense of it all. My childhood attempts to ignore these hurtful feelings (such as the time that my white guidance counselor at my black junior high school, explicitly told me that I would never get into Townsend Harris, so don't bother applying) no longer worked. Without consciously realizing it, keeping up with the USEM readings and assignments became emotionally unbearable and I started falling behind in Professor Sundiata's course.

I will never forget the day the professor kept calling on me in class, because he just knew that I had something to contribute. Embarrassed, I repeatedly hung my head and said, "I don't know." At one point, he appeared to give me a bewildered look as if to say, "What happened?" and I, too, began wondering the same thing. I made it a point to meet with him after class in his office to see what excuse I could muster up to explain my predicament.

Before I could address his disappointment of my dismal performance in class that day and beg for his forgiveness, I was completely taken aback when instead I started bawling and found myself exclaiming, "Professor, they hate me here!" To my surprise, he did not dismiss my sudden outburst as an overreaction or admonish me to focus on the matter at hand, which of course were my studies. Instead, he immediately jumped up (as if he KNEW this was coming!), handed me a box of tissues, gently patted my shoulder and in a very calm manner said, "Now, now. Settle down." He proceeded to tell me about all of the women of color over the years who sat exactly where I sat, and their narratives of overcoming, all the while reassuring me that I, too, would work through these Brandeis challenges.

What I found in Professor Sundiata from that moment was a refuge, someone I could feel safe with. At one of the lowest and most uncertain points in my life, Professor Sundiata was a stable and guiding force that assured me that he was not letting go until he was confident that I had found sure footing for myself on the other side of victory. He never imposed his perspectives on me and was always there to listen and provide guidance as often as I needed it. Never was I turned down when I found myself in desperation at his office door or when I called. In a word, Professor Sundiata was and is my champion.

After graduating Brandeis a semester early, I went on to obtain a Master of Urban Planning from New York University's Robert F. Wagner School of Public Service. As life would have it, I was in my final semester of my program when a devastating 7.0 earthquake struck my Haitian homeland on January 12, 2010. Here I was, yet again, at a turning point where I had to address the centrality of my identity and my newfound career trajectory. This time, a dynamic man by the name of Mitchell Silver emerged and much like Professor Sundiata, continues to have a profound influence on my development as a person and as an emerging professional.

I met Mitch four months before the earthquake at an annual conference that the New York Metro Chapter of the American Planning Association (APA) was hosting in September 2009. I was a student speaker at the conference where I had the privilege of discussing my experience as policy consultant with New York City's

Office of Financial Empowerment and how my urban planning background came to bear on this particular role. Apparently, Mitch had also spoken at the conference because by the time we got to the banquet luncheon, every speaker that took the podium lauded him at the start of his or her remarks. At one point, the crowd of hundreds gave him a standing ovation. When I stood on the tip of my toes and realized that this was a black man, I just knew I had to talk to him somehow.

According to a recent APA survey, the urban planning profession in the United States of America is about two percent black. Even without the survey, my lived experience revealed this to me, as a colleague and I were the two black urban planning students in our class of about sixty students. Ironically, her specialization was in international planning and mine was more domestically oriented in housing and economic policy. Throughout graduate school, it was common for me to attend student gatherings comprised of the five major urban planning programs in the New York City region and be the only black individual in crowds of about hundred students. Prior to my run-in with Mitch, I had never met a black male urban planner and was only aware of one black woman in the profession at the time.

As soon as the luncheon ended, I located Mitch and ran down the hall making my way through the crowds towards his direction. When I caught up to him, I breathlessly and hastily muttered, "Hi. My name is Vanessa Leon and I am a second-year planner at NYU, Wagner." In my mission to get to him, I had not actually thought through what I would say and started to feel a bit silly now that I had caught up to him and was standing there nervously gasping for air. Mitch graciously redeemed me by expressing how much our field needed young visionaries like me.

Without me having to say a word, it is as if he knew why I chased him down and the type of mentoring I was craving from a professional who looked like me. He gave me his card and no matter how busy he was, he would always provide thorough responses to my email updates and questions over the following months.

Unbeknownst to me, the whole time I was corresponding with him, he was the first black president-elect in the history of the American Planning Association. The more Mitch and I got to know one another, the more we were both taken aback by the similarities between us. Mitch's tireless drive and passion for healthy people and communities across the globe empowered me to expand my worldview, as I, too, looked to positively shape the built environments that people live and work in.

Unlike Professor Sundiata, it was clear for me from the beginning that Mitch was my mentor. I did not know how bad I needed Professor Sundiata initially, but with Mitch, I knew right away. I was purposeful and determined in cultivating my relationship with Mitch so that I could explore how I might learn as much as possible from him in order to grow as much as I could professionally. The trail that he blazed for rising planners like myself fascinated me and inspired me to see past societal or organizational limitations that were being placed on me as I looked to carve out a path of my own.

A mentor is someone who walks alongside another while providing strategic guidance along the way. It is my belief that a promising mentor/mentee relationship is a joint investment. From this perspective, the mentor invests their time and energy into the growth of the mentee and the mentee consequently reciprocates by demonstrating that he or she is receptive to the valued insights of the mentor and actually willing to apply and expand upon what he or she is gleaning from the relationship. In this way, the mentee ensures that the mentor is making good on their investment while also being conscious of opportunities that may present themselves for the mentee to become a mentor to another.

Additionally, I firmly believe that it is the responsibility of the mentee to provide the mentor with material to work off of particularly in a professional mentoring relationship. Both mentor and mentee stand to benefit when the mentee has an idea of the direction he or she would like their career to progress, even when answers to questions such as 'how to get there?' and 'how long will it take?' are not readily apparent. Knowing that the mentee has a vision enables the mentor to be more deliberate with presenting the mentee with opportunities that the mentee was not aware of otherwise, or assist the mentee with brainstorming in a way that may not have necessarily been intuitive to the mentee.

This is precisely what characterizes my relationship with Mitch. In the weeks and months following the Haiti earthquake, I did not know how to contend with the disheartening reality that over 230,000 of my Haitian brothers and sisters perished in 35 seconds – not because of an earthquake but rather – as a result of the collapse of buildings that should have never been built the way they were or where they stood prior to this unfortunate occurrence. Born to a beautiful Haitian mother and a father of German descent, Mitch intimately understood my bewilderment and held my hand as I struggled to literally and figuratively make my way through the rubble that had completely upended my post-graduation plans and the course of my life.

Currently, my very make-up as a Haitian-American urban planner influences everything I do through Pinchina Consulting, the international urban planning firm that I since founded to actively partake in Haiti's long-term redevelopment process. I know without a doubt that I would not have had the fortitude that I have today to take on this difficult work had it not been for the foundation that Professor Sundiata laid and that Mitch continually reinforces with his support. Professor Sundiata taught me that I am part of a larger story while showing me how to embrace my unique narrative within that story. Mitch humbly taught me how to be an urban planner with courage. He assured me that I could harmoniously bridge the gap between who I am as a person and what I do as a professional in order to affect lasting change for the most vulnerable among us.

I find it interesting in retrospect that my most formative mentoring relationships developed with really strong and supportive black men. To some extent, I wonder whether this was somehow a subconscious attempt to make up for the shortcomings that I might have had in my relationship with my father. My dad's love for me has always been present even when he did not do the best job of conveying it always, or in displaying it in a way that resonated with me. What was often lacking from my dad was direction in terms of making my way in the world as I came into my own. Professor Ibrahim Sundiata and Mitchell Silver, therefore, without any of us explicitly realizing it, rose to the occasion in providing me with critical male guidance at really transformative and transitional periods of my life as I navigated the uncertainty, the insecurities and the fear that accompanied the early challenges that I faced as a young adult. More recently, I have been blessed with the privilege of working with and learning from vibrant and impactful women, the likes of Ms. Barbara Ann Perkins, who I first met as a 2014 fellow of the highly selective Master's Series for Distinguished Leaders program. Ms. Barbara and a few of my other female mentors are helping me achieve greater life/work balance even as my career continues to soar.

As I commit to operating within the urban planning profession to make the world a little less rough and a whole lot smoother for those traversing through life with me, as well as for those to follow, I am constantly reminded of my high school Ephebic Oath where I vowed "to not leave my city any less, but rather greater than I found it." Though I embarked on my career with a very timid belief of whether this was possible, I am forever indebted to my mentors for not only coming into my life to show me that this is possible but for actively engaging me in the process of making it possible.

The Magic of **MENTORING**

PEARLS *of* WISDOM

Section Three

Cheryl Brownlee
CEO, CB Communications
SILENT WARRIOR

*Mentor - someone willing to share their life journey by passing
on to others as a blessing to be cherished with the hope to
make a difference or positive impact in someone else's life.
Silent Warrior embraces courage, compassion, discipline and
training to master one's own alter ego.*

My journey began at a young age learning to survive. I was sexually abused and raped at an early age by a close family friend at 16. These incidents would shape my life forever in the decisions I made.

Choosing not to be a victim, I took on the role of caregiver, a go-to person always there for others. If you did that, of course you would be loved/liked and the horrific pain that was suppressed deep down in my soul never exposed. Shhhh… never talk about it or you will embarrass the family and who would believe you?

My grandmother was a radiant soul that I looked up to often. She was the first person that I can remember that mentored me. She always seemed to know the right things to say. I remember she told me when I was little to live by God's Golden Rule and you will be okay, "Treat people the way you want to be treated." She said it's not going to be easy, but have faith and know God has your back. Remember family first and never disgrace the family name. Through the years I strived so hard to model that behavior. Thinking in my mind, "What a concept! Everyone should know that rule!" so I simply applied it without receiving the same.

It was confusing to people out there who are different and think differently. She taught me the true meaning of CARE (**C**uddle, **A**dore,

Respect, Enjoy) your family, that's all you have. That's where you receive your joy. My mother taught me the meaning of self-preservation. She always said, "If you take care of yourself first, then you can give to others. It's okay to give, but not at the risk of sacrificing who you are."

My mom is the one person in my life that I know for sure that has loved me totally and completely unconditionally. Mom always describes me as the daughter that would give the shirt off her back to anyone. I was too trusting and always giving, not recognizing who I was, and sometimes I was giving back to myself in friendship and relationships. I was so busy giving and trying to make sure everyone else was okay, that I didn't give anyone a chance to give to me.

I've had some incredible mentors early in my life and continue to have, but like most people, I probably didn't realize the value and the precious advice that could have saved me from a lot of my not-so good choices/decisions. People that I have known 25 years and more that have molded me and shaped me into the person that I am today deserve a quick shout out; Cindy, Wanda, Kathy, Inger, Vanessa, Kim, Pat, Cathy, Gwiin, Darlessia, Nadine, Kathryn, Lindy and Wanda L., to name a few. You see, to me, mentoring goes both ways; it is someone you can learn from, and someone to learn with in good times and sometimes not so good times. It is the lesson you receive and you sharing that lesson, which makes mentoring one of life's special lessons. You see, sometimes you can be a mentor from afar and people might not know that the words, thoughts or deeds that they have shared can make a lasting impression in your life. These women and others have given me the quote I often use, "Communicate, Advocate, Reflect, Educate (equals CARE), and lead by example."

The love of my life and most precious blessing has been my son, Kenny, who is my best friend and the person I am most proud of. He brings me joy every day and gives me the reason for living, and to get up every morning and continue to be a silent warrior. He has given me an opportunity to serve another special young man in my life, my grandson Rhys, to push me to think about my legacy. You see, mentoring goes both ways, because through my son and grandson I become the mentee.

I met Barbara Perkins almost eight years ago. I will never forget her smile and the incredible hug I so willingly received. I met her through another mentor, Marcia Dyson. Barbara instantly knew how to grab my heart. It was the last night at the Congressional Black Caucus and she came up to me and put her arms around me and said, "Sugar, I have something for you." It was the book "Sisters at the Well." This one relationship took my life through a whirlwind that I haven't stopped feeling even now. She speaks about how she had the opportunity to sit at the feet of the great Dorothy Heights. I have had an amazing opportunity to sit front row center in her life. She has taught me the true meaning of "mentoring." Mentoring is something you live, eat and breathe. It's the wake-up call at 4 a.m. in the morning when you just want to turn over and get the last sleep, but instead you listen and sometimes advise the person on the other end of the phone. It's the time you are driving in a car for miles and no one speaks, but you are there allowing the person to feel the support, love, and peace. It's the time you don't want to hear what the person is going to say because it might not be loving talk, but the hard truth. It's your daily work. This is God's work.

Throughout your day, every day, you are mentoring someone. Whether it's your family, friends, everyday folk, you are modeling behavior that someone is going to take and use.

Psalms 119:24 – *Thy testimonies are my delight and my counsellors.*

"Have an absolutely fabulous day" and remember, "When you've been blessed, pass it on."

Theresa Price
Founder, National College Resource Foundation
I Believe in You

I was born in a time where our parents fought for equal rights and we saw our elders "fight for what they believed in." We took pride in standing for something, fighting for something, and believing in something. This generation doesn't see and feel what we did, so they are less aggressive, and it seems as though as opportunities are more available, students seem less enthused about taking advantage of those opportunities. If you think about it, we were mentored to take a stand and take advantage of all opportunities. Something has been lost along the way as we see a majority of our youth not built with the same "machinery." With that said, mentoring from us, the "old school", is needed and a must to be passed on to the "new school."

Life is about leaving a legacy for the next generation of something that we as individuals stood for, something that we did that left an impression on someone's life or what we did for others. Mentoring allows us to touch our young people who will become America's next leaders. As we look at our young people today, especially our young people of color, and even further, our African American youth, mentoring is needed now more than ever. This era seems to be full of misguided, social, emotional, Foster and at-risk youth that are in need of direction and support towards positive post-secondary pathways.

Our low resource students, particularly African American kids and Black males, are being punished more, labeled more and really pushed in a corner, where they have no fight in them, because they are constantly being told what they are not, and that they are less than. We, as current stakeholders in our communities, must provide direction, guidance, and encouragement for our young people and that's why "mentoring" is key. Mentoring requires us to spend valuable time with our young people, to share positive words, spread love to them, support, guidance, encouragement and the necessity to seek a higher education. Though it is known that we can't help everyone, we need to do what we can in the circle that we have and the surroundings that we can reach. Understanding that this generation grew up in an era of - I will use the expression - "freedom," no more belts, no church in the schools, everyone gets to play on the team regardless of talent, and everybody gets a trophy, whether it was deserved or not. This created an "It's all about ME world."

Young people now feel they are entitled to everything, even though they may be just beginning their quest. But we must understand, it's not their fault. They are growing up as "Net" babies. They were born when the Internet already existed, plus we have drive-thru coffee shops, drive-thru banks, and believe it or not, even drive-thru churches, and mortuaries. So what do we expect? This is where mentoring can help change the thought process, or at least develop a greater sense of understanding about the importance of elevating one's game, and why higher education is so important. We have to help young people understand the concept of crawling before they walk when they in fact almost came out running, if you look at technology. They know "push," "enter," "app," but are far removed from the three words we had to know and had to live by, "hello," "please," and "thank you", plus the importance of looking people in the eyes when you speak.

I am blessed that I was mentored by wonderful teachers, community leaders, and a supportive family. Being the youngest of 9 children, all that love made me want to give love to others. I love helping others and helping young people believe in themselves. There is nothing more rewarding than seeing a person who didn't believe they could do something, and then they blossomed into something great, because you provided some love and support, and a touch of encouraging words. And that's why it is the magic of mentoring and "Mentoring is a Must!" As we help young people, they will discover the hidden treasure that God placed in each of us here for a purpose. Heck, it took me almost 50 years to even realize that God has each of us here for a purpose, and when we discover our purpose, that purpose is directly tied to our prosperity. Passion, Purpose and Prosperity are the three "P's" of a promising life. This is where the core of my mentorship comes from as I relate to young people every day.

I truly want our young people to know that they are loved, needed and wanted, and with faith in God, ALL things are possible. So, as I mentor young people every day, my theory for them and belief in them is my message, "So I say to you, young people, spread your wings and fly like an eagle in the sky! Fly so high and never stop until you reach that mountaintop."

Alva Adams-Mason
National Manager, African American Business Strategy, Toyota USA
GIVE WHAT YOU WOULD LIKE
TO RECEIVE

Growing up in the South in Ft. Lauderdale, FL as the oldest of six children, mentoring was really important to me. My father, Ellie Adams, never completed college and my mother, Ella Webb-Adams, never had a chance to go. Unfortunately, I lost my mother at the young age of 15 during a time where it was important to have the guidance, support and unconditional love of your mother. Her last words were, "God, please take care of my kids." I always remember her powerful statement in my day-to-day doings, work and dealings with people. So far, all of her prayers have been answered. It was the end of my freshman year in high school, and I remember at the end of her funeral running after her casket saying, "Mom don't worry about me. I am going to be okay and go to college." My Mom had planned on going to college when she got pregnant with me. Then, my father went on to college, but ended up coming back home due to family pressure, because he had a lot of children to take care of and needed to get a job to take care of the family; thus, he didn't finish. I knew that going to college was always a dream for both of my parents.

I was very involved in high school. I remember this guidance counselor named Mrs. Pratt. She was African American. Going back to elementary school, I started out in segregated schools and by the time I was in fifth grade, I was being bussed out to what I considered a majority white school. My first teacher was Mrs. Erma Allen, who always had positive stuff to say about being successful and doing your work. When I finally started high school, I realized I really needed someone to help me because I did not understand the process of getting into college or what to do. Mrs. Pratt, the guidance counselor, stepped in and said, "You're going to college and this is what you need to do…" That probably was the beginning to really understanding how important it was for someone to mentor and guide me. Another woman named Mrs. Gail Davis came over to me at the time and said, "You know you're going to be a debutant and I am going to help you." I had all these women that came out of nowhere who knew that I did not have a mom and saw that I possessed the potential to become something great. To them, being great was going to college and graduating. I seemed to always have a guardian angel. I find that it instills confidence right away when someone who cares about you tells you what you are going to do rather than allowing you to waiver in indecision.

Through all of that, I realized how important it was for me to do the same. I mentor because I always give what I want to receive in return, from a mental standpoint. I give love and I give mentoring because I would want that girl who is standing out there feeling lost, in need of love and encouragement, to know you can achieve what you desire. I am especially moved when a girl or woman is doing all the work they are supposed to do, but they just need specific guidance or resources to connect them to people or networks that I now have access to. It is worth stopping to make time to listen.

Mentoring is a process that involves communication. It is relationship-based, and you have to build trust. I find that my mentoring base is with young African American women. It's because I have three daughters. I am constantly mentoring them to give them words of wisdom, so they don't have to step in the puddles I stepped into. Then there are women in other organizations or who work around me that need to have that reassurance and confidence instilled in them by someone who can tell or show them what they can do with what they have. With all the different things that go on in our country, African American girls and women are not recognized or valued the way they should be, which is why mentoring them is important to me.

If I have to be the advocate to get them to where they need to be, then I guess that is me. Everybody has different talents. Usually, in dealing with African American girls and women it is our own lack of self-esteem that gets in our way. You just need someone to let you know you're okay and remind you of the super-power you hold within. So much of what we second-guess ourselves on, is psychological. At the end and beginning of the day, it is our responsibility to help each other.

In my position, I come up with constant strategies for Toyota to make an important impact in the African American community, so that the African American community understands that we are not just selling cars. Toyota is the number one car among African American consumers, and our goal is to enhance our reputation and maintain our relationship in the community.

Until now, I admit that in my professional life I had some struggles and moments where low confidence showed up. I got married at 26 and was divorced by 36 with three children. It was hard trying to financially and emotionally survive, feeling like a social misfit in the community while being a single parent and having strong, yet clear, career aspirations. I credit my survivorship to prayer and growing up in a praying family. Prayer was a ritual for my grandmothers.

Knowing that nothing could stop me but myself, I continued to walk through the hard times, work and do what I needed to do, knowing that things would somehow come to fruition. My strong point, I was never going to give up, and I did not. Now I see how that was all good. You will have tough times, but you have to believe, have faith, discipline and focused work ethics to pull you through. Perseverance has always been my strongest attribute. This holds true in my professional experience as well. Yes, I had people I could call for advice, but I never really had anyone inside the company that mentored me.

In reality, one of the difficulties for African American women in Corporate America is open and direct access to getting a mentor.

The list of available Black women mentors is thin within companies. The best professional advice I received has been from white males. Although, in my current position, my boss is a Black male and he has helped me a lot and pushed for me to get the job that I now have. The truth is, I have had some great bosses and some bad ones. There was no guide on "How To Emotionally Handle Bad Bosses." Unfortunately, most of what I have learned has been through trial and error. There was a brief time when I had a mentor, who was the President of Toyota Financial Services, who told me "Alva, when you want something, walk in and ask for it; that's what men do." It was very important for me to learn how to protect myself from bad bosses and equally imperative to learn how to capitalize off a boss when they really liked you and before they were gone.

The main reason I mentor other girls and women is because I experienced a dire need myself. There are so many young people in need of the right kind of help who could use my talent, knowledge and constructive advice to take them to the next level in life. I recall meeting Barbara Perkins, a mentor and coach. We ran into each other at an event and decided to get together one day. When we did, we had so much in common and connected really well. I sensed that she came into my life for a reason and was yet another angel sent to give me guidance and mentorship.

On the other hand, when I make time to speak with individuals, I expect for mentees to be real serious about what they ask for, possess confidence and follow through. The main thing is that once you're successful with the mentoring you have received, it is your duty to pay it forward by mentoring someone else.

I believe you truly do the world a favor when you mentor someone, especially the next generation.

Darrell Brown
Senior Vice President, U.S. Bank
THE NECESSITIES OF MENTORSHIP

Her name was Ms. Carol, my fifth grade teacher, who created imagery and excitement with each word spoken on the many topics or subjects she taught. On reflection, her knowledge was vast and her vocabulary immense, yet she always operated within my personal sphere of understanding, comprehension and language acumen, all qualities a good mentor must embrace. Because of her I became an active listener and an accomplished student. She engaged within me a condition of interested attention on all topics and I quickly became a willing learner of her teaching. She had the unique gift of awakening the yearning brilliance that resides within each of us.

Ms. Carol changed the course of my history and thus the quality of my personal and professional career, particularly as it related to my role as advisor, consultant, coach, teacher and mentor. What was her secret? What gift did she possess?

Well, Ms. Carol did more than teach. She helped her students learn! This is a subtle yet powerful difference and I still live and breathe the residue of that difference. She was masterful at the art of asking questions to confirm understanding of her lessons. She would recognize and celebrate the emergence of new thoughts and broadened understanding. She encouraged a dialogue, not a monologue, and at a young age, I felt the value of being heard, which for a student of any age is immeasurable. Ms. Carol's teaching and her learning principles are a metaphor for mentorship.

Mentorship in its simplest form is the communication of experience. This experience may consist of facts, truths, ideas, or ideals, or it may consist of processes, skills, talents or competencies. It is the shaping of thought and understanding to the comprehension of the mentee, the cultivation of one's capacity and the transmission of experience, which make up the mentor's work.

As a Senior Vice President for a major bank, I've made mentorship a cornerstone of leadership development. The mentor's job is to help the mentee understand where they should go, where they can go, and then how to get there. The mentor plays a critical role in helping the mentee cross the bridge from information to knowledge and the meaning of things begins to emerge. During the mentorship interaction, questions are asked and answers are sought and the mentor should challenge the mentee while providing guidance and encouragement. A mentor should help the mentee to believe in him or herself and boost their confidence.

The urge to be accountable to someone as a mentor is indeed a gift, and to know that beyond the mentee there is an answer that must be given and cannot be denied. Out of such an experience a new and fresh perspective emerges and the primary mission becomes that of achievement and higher levels of accomplishment. Mentors help mentees develop a clear vision for their career path with persistence, determination, endurance, fortitude, tolerance, and courage to take action while bringing their vision to fruition. Yet progress in a form requires constant effort, for obstacles exist that might discourage some. Life is designed to be a story of achievement in spite of adversity, not in the absence of adversity. A great mentor will help someone navigate the trapdoors and landmines of corporate America. The act of mentorship is in part an act of comparing and judging or finding something in past experiences that will explain and make meaningful the new learning experience.

Over the years I've had many mentors and they each possessed an outstanding ability to explain and teach. They helped people identify their strengths and weaknesses while delivering feedback directly and constructively. They also possessed the ability to inspire and lead people to discover their own answers. Mentorship should be looked upon as the foundation of personal and professional development capable of transforming people and organizations from the alleys of mediocrity to the peaks of achievement. Mentorship, capsulated truth, uniqueness and individuality and will clearly identify guidelines for those in search of a better life and for those seeking discovery of themselves.

I've not seen Ms. Carol in over fifty years, but her legacy lives, and I'm honored to share her story and give you a glimpse into her teaching methodology, which provides the essence of teaching, the art of learning, and the value of mentorship.

Erica Walden
Attorney/Professor
CoNfidENCE RENEWEd

I have never had a formal mentor. When others spoke about their mentors, I often felt a twinge of jealousy as if I had been left out of an exclusive club or society. But finding a mentor is not something that you can set about doing, like a task on a "to-do" list. I know this because I have tried to find a mentor that way. My search was just like the chapter, "Are you my mentor?" in Sheryl Sandberg's book, Lean In. I was wandering around looking for someone to be my go-to guide. I have never found that person.

Even though I have not been blessed to have that one "guru-like" mentor relationship, I have had several people mentor me at key points in my life.

When I began my career of practicing law, I was assigned to a terrible Partner. I know that I am smart, but knowing the law and practicing the law are two very different things. I needed to be taught how to practice the law. He gave me no guidance and threw me under the bus when it was time for my performance review. I was shocked and devastated by what happened. I wanted to quit, but that would admit defeat, which I was unwilling to do. It would also mean that I had no income to pay off my enormous student loan debt.

Fortunately, my secretary rallied for me. She helped me compose myself and she sought out a different Partner to guide me. With their help I was able to regroup. I learned how to practice law and how to do my job well. Still, that first experience shook my confidence and I eventually left the firm.

From that experience over a decade ago to the present, I have had wonderful men and women see my value and take time out of their lives to help direct my path. I found Barbara Perkins along one such path. We were both invited to the home of a mutual friend. This friend had gathered together women from different facets of her life: lifelong friends and their friends, her mentees, former colleagues and their mentees. It was a wonderful gathering of women who may never have met each other, but for this gathering, and had so much to share with one another.

When Barbara arrived, positive energy was radiating from her and I was drawn to her. I didn't seek out a mentoring relationship. I merely wanted to know her. And knowing her has made such a difference in my life.

From that first experience practicing law until recently, I have felt extremely incompetent in my law practice. I eventually left the practice of law and enjoyed a new career in real estate development. I was very good at my job and very confident in my new career. But Barbara kept introducing me as a lawyer. She kept soliciting my help for a variety of legal tasks. She believed that I was competent, even though my faith in my skills had been shaken.

Eventually, because of economic challenges, I was forced to dust-off my legal license and return to the very career that gave me knots in my stomach, and it was Barbara who introduced me to the person who is mentoring me through this next phase of my life.

My current mentor has helped to renew my faith in my abilities as an attorney. He has directed me through difficult tasks and encouraged me when I became discouraged. He has also introduced me to a new career as a professor. He is a professor and felt that teaching is something that I would also be good at.

At first I rejected the suggestion. I did not believe that I knew enough or that I would be able to do the job. However, with his persistence and reassurance I have embarked upon a new career, which I love.

I feel competent and fulfilled. I no longer have knots in my stomach when I go to work. I am proud of my new career and I am confident in my abilities. Having someone recognize your talent, encourage you to pursue endeavors that you believe are beyond your abilities, guide you through challenges along your path, and motivate you when you are in doubt that is the power of mentoring.

This new career has also given me an opportunity to mentor others. My students ask me questions about life and career opportunities. I am very happy to provide them with encouragement and direction to help them succeed.

So, mentoring for me has not been one "go-to" person for my journey. It has been a variety of different men and women who have guided me at various stages along the way. Each has provided essential advice and direction that has ultimately led me to the place where I am now, and I am grateful to each one of them.

Dawn Sutherland
Retired Corporate Executive/Philanthropist
A PATHWAY TO SUCCESS

My mother was my first mentor. For so many people, their first mentor in life is their mother. From the first time that we open our eyes, our very first image is our mother. In the beginning stages of life, our mothers are our everything, our God if you will, until we are old enough to learn that God is a spirit, a higher life force, which created our mothers and is also our guiding light. My mother taught me that I could do anything. At an early age, she felt that by sending me to board with high-powered relatives and to boarding school, I would be in an excellent learning environment, conducive to meeting people and being around like-minded youth, thus placing me on a pathway to success. My mother was preparing me for the guidance of mentors. I was taught by my mother to create an environment for myself where I would surround myself with people who are positive, productive, and reciprocal in friendship.

Did I make mention that I am the baby child of seven siblings? My mother gave birth to me at the age of fifty. My sister, may she rest in peace, was my second mother. Can you imagine having five brothers and one sister, all of who were old enough to be your parent? As my siblings can attest, they spoiled me rotten!

Mother said, "Move far away from the Bronx so that if anyone wants to visit you, they can't just drop in!" and, "Get three good women friends, because they will be there for you always – even after your husband is dead!" Betty Arnold, Vice President at Xerox Corporation, Barbara Perkins, President at Image Builders Etcetera, Deidra Williams, Vice President at Xerox Corporation, Avis Frazier-Thomas, Vice President at Warner Bros., and Marie Deary, Wealth Management Finance Advisors, INC. – Each woman has played an integral part in my professional and personal life. Although I never married, I must say, "Mother you were so right about having three - I have five! - good friends as a support system!"

My first professional mentor was Don C. Burr. In 1982, when I joined Xerox Corporation, just after earning my MBA from Clark Atlanta University, Xerox Corporation implemented a Directed Development Mentorship Program. I was assigned a mentor, Don C. Burr, who was VP of Finance, Xerox Corporation, and several pay grades ahead of me at the time. I am thankful to Don C. Burr for mentoring me. I met with Don C. Burr every Friday for years – even after the initial mentor agreed upon time was over.

You see, Don had a purpose. He would invite me to meet people of all walks of life, introducing me to people who were from a wide range of social/economic levels. Etiquette was on Don's Top 10 list – so-to-speak - and I appreciated his candor. Always giving me constructive criticism, Don was concerned about how I mixed and mingled with various groups of people.

Remember, I was straight out of the Bronx, and I did not bite my tongue. Sometimes that kind of behavior can put people off. If one isn't careful, things truly can get lost in translation – believe me.

As a result, Don gave his wife the assignment of making sure that as I moved forward in this world, I would have no issues with class/race/global thoughts and opinions, when and wherever I entered.

My mentor, Brian Stern – Vice President of Finance, Xerox Corporation, also played a pivotal role in my career, giving me an opportunity to move to the UK and work for Xerox Corporation in Finance in England.

When I arrived on the scene, working in Finance, there were very few women in that sector of business. But I was not deterred, breaking barriers for women, taking care of business, knocking 'em out of the box!

My most notable mentor, Ursula Burns, current CEO of Xerox Corporation, always told me early on in my career, "Always be technically competent and focused and success will come."

The years that Suzi Good, Vice President, General Manager, Global Account Operations at Xerox Corporation, mentored me are some of the most memorable experiences. I had moved to California and the sunshine and beaches served as a nice backdrop to a very busy schedule in Century City, CA.

Liz Stafford, President, Inland Business Systems at Xerox Corporation, Betty Arnold, Vice President at Xerox Corporation, Deidra Williams, Vice President at Xerox Corporation, Avis Frazier-Thomas, Vice President at Warner Bros., Marie Deary, Wealth Management Finance Advisors, INC., are remarkable women that live in the present, managing their families and full books of business, and are constantly breaking barriers for women. Hats off to you, Ladies!

Mentoring is a selfless act that benefits both the mentor and the mentee. Early on in my career I saw the importance of mentoring people who worked for me, because at one point in time, I would learn as much as possible, making myself indispensable, so when I was told of another opportunity to move forward my boss would say, "Dawn, we can't afford to replace you!"

Oh, I learned. After having the experience of being "indispensable," I realized that if I didn't train someone to step into my place, I would be pigeonholed into a position, and simply not be promoted. Hold up – wait a minute! I fixed that.

I started training people so well until when it came time for me to step on up to the next phase of my career and my boss said, "We can't afford to replace you!" I could with confidence say to my boss, "I have a replacement identified." – BINGO!

Although I haven't given birth to children, I have truly been blessed to mentor plenty of nieces, nephews, co-workers, college students and myriads of other people's children. Over the years, I have had plenty of opportunity to help push our youth forward. It's been so rewarding to see so many young men and women from the USA and Africa, matriculate through universities around the USA.

Throughout the age of time, I shall only wish that my mentees and others know the positive effects of mentoring. We as mentors can alter lives in so many positive ways; helping people to see that providing light, a pathway for our youth, actually serves the universe.

To date, I have retired from XEROX Corporation (early) – moved from Los Angeles, CA, and am currently living my life/dream in Kumasi, Ghana. I am fearlessly living in the present, building a strong foundation, providing a pathway and a light for the women who still have a glimmer of faith, knowing that tomorrow the sun will rise, a new day will come. I know that by being equipped with proper knowledge and then applying the newly gained knowledge, tomorrow will be a better day.

Reflecting on the words of the late Ruby Dee, *"In those little flashes of moments...that picks us up from some moments of despair."* That is how I would like to be remembered.

Aubry Stone
President/CEO, CA Black Chamber of Commerce
Operate and Excel At 100%
Even on a Rainy Day

I escaped New York with a lot of prayers. I was surrounded by conflict. Thankfully, I had many positive forces in my life. One day, a bell went off in my head and I had to think to myself, is what I am about to do going to embarrass my parents? Eventually, I knew that I had to make changes if I wanted to not disappoint my family. Quite honestly, when I realized I needed to make different decisions for myself, a mentor showed up.

My first mentor was my music teacher Mr. Emanuel, back in the 7th to 9th grade. Obviously, I saw him every day and he really took a liking to me. He saw something in me that I did not see. He encouraged me to try things in music that I did not think were possible, including taking a test to get accepted into a high school for music and art, the same school from the hit television show called, FAME. It was the most famous high school in New York City. I thought it was ridiculous, but not Mr. Emanuel. At that time, I considered his mentorship as being more of a role model; not only in his dress and encouragement, but the way he carried himself and his demeanor. Mr. Emanuel taught me how to be respectful towards adults and have adult conversations with my contemporaries. This was all-important to me growing up, because it helped me navigate in a world that I was trying to grasp and understand in order for me to become a better person.

In a lot of situations, in a minority community, there may be positive people in your life like your aunts or other family members, but they may not have the knowledge of your academic or creative skill set. Conversely, I comprehend the importance for many professional mentors to assist me. Now I take pride in the fact that I get my greatest love from inspiring others and being a teacher. If in some way what I do creates an opportunity for mentorship, then I guess I do consider myself a mentor. I think being a mentor is a much-esteemed position. In my case, I find that I'm not only giving advice to one or two people, but many across the country whenever I can. They don't have to be a member of the California Black Chamber of Commerce. I have never turned anyone down, and if I have, I do apologize. It is important to me to especially help men of color who have a difficult time in finding male relationships with people they can talk to and grow.

In 1978, I served my last military assignment in the U.S. Air Force and I chose to stay in California instead of going back to Brooklyn, NY. I told myself that I could operate at 100-miles an hour here in Sacramento, CA and excel. I was right. I created a good life and I desire the same for others.

My life is interesting. I did 24 years in the U.S. Air Force, which lends itself to an affirming sense of "do whatever it takes" attitude. I came out into the civilian world with the same attitude and mindset that if I have to work 23-hours a day to get something done, then that is what I will do. It carried over into my professional career and lifestyle. I don't believe in excuses. Function wise, I had a lot of self-discipline to make things happen. It was a natural thing in the military to see projects through from beginning to completion. This type of work ethic is what I feel needs to be emphasize in our next generation of leaders.

Coming to the Chamber was somewhat accidental. Previously I was in the corporate world moving through marketing and sales ranks relatively fast. I became a Vice President of a large insurance company with about 30 people working for me. It was not a big deal because in the military, I had 500 people working for me. The mindset was different because the 30 corporate workers wanted to make money, but the military personnel just wanted to "get out." While running my division at the insurance company, I got on the Board of the local

Chamber of Commerce in Sacramento, CA. The attitude I took then is the same attitude I have now, if you're not going to be a part of the solution, then you're obviously a part of the problem. I started solving problems and building solutions. Instead of backing away, I became more entrenched and served as the President for three years. During my tenure as President from 1991 to 1993, we elected to start a statewide organization in order to tie the activities of the chambers together and have a stronger voice in the state capitol. Afterwards, I was asked to be the President/CEO. I agreed to fill the position for six months until they found someone else. That was 21 years ago, and I am still the President/CEO of the California Black Chamber of Commerce. I guess I am doing a good job.

When it comes to my success, sadly the standards of influence did not happen in my professional circles. There wasn't really that one person who stood out and recognized my talent and skills. However, the seeds of mentorship that encouraged me to go to college came through the guidance of my uncle when I was 18 years old. This is why I am so adamant about mentoring now because I did not have that in the Chamber or corporate world.

There have been plenty of days where I had to mentor myself and make tough decisions. My interpretation of a mentor is someone who is just a telephone call away whenever you need them, and no such person existed for me.

This particular point leads me to where I am today, because out of all the things that I have done, the thing I wish for the most is to have had someone I could have looked up to and they took time out to be a mentor on speed-dial in my own life. This is why it is important to help people on their journey. I have been helped and I have assisted many others in actualizing their businesses and building their dreams.

Another person who comes to mind when encouraging people to be their best representative is Barbara Perkins, a uniquely talented lady that I have grown to truly admire. She is a backroom General. She has humbleness about her and goes methodically about what she does. She is definitely a gladiator. We have spoken on each other's panels, as advocates for right or wrong, and I can always count on Barbara to give it her best shot. This is what mentors do!

In my crazy imagination, as a late bloomer, I am very happy and proud of my life; however, had I had a mentor in my life, who knows, I may have been a State Senator or something. Really, I encourage individuals, no matter what environment you are in (corporate, non-profit, politics) to seek out a person you hold in high esteem and don't be bashful to ask them to be your mentor. Be bold! If they got your interest, there is a high probability that they will say, "Yes!"

The most necessary factor involved and critical point in mentoring is to meet mentees where they are in their lives without superficially imposing your title and who you are. If you impose your position it can create a communication barrier and blockage in their life. Typically, individuals want to be and do better, but need assistance in getting to where they want to be. This way you demonstrate empathy in their current situation.

Remember to not be afraid to make mistakes, and when you do - because you will - apologize for it, learn from the experience and move forward. There is not a lot of room for the weak-hearted. In our environment you have to be aggressive, stay focused and not be afraid to act on your instincts when you believe that what you're doing is right.

Kellie Hawkins
Health Policy Analyst
AWAKENING POTENTIAL,
THE POWER of MENTORING

"I am not a teacher, but an awakener." Robert Frost

Mentors awaken our potential to be the best at our craft. I have been fortunate to have these "awakeners" known as mentors throughout my career of public service. While they have been primarily African American women, I have a myriad of mentors ranging from college professors to women in the community I admire for their tact, motivations, and contribution to the community and their field. In my role as a policy advisor on national health investments, I find myself recalling the pearls of wisdom through my mentors. These words usually help reinforce a decision I am making or get me to re-calibrate my approach to ensure the true intent of my work is present.

My mentors represent multiple sectors from government to corporate America. So the diversity of thought is ever present at all times. I also am reassured daily that I am not walking alone and I have a support system that spans beyond my parents who laid the initial foundation for my development.

Carolyn Webb de Macias - My Mentor

One of the first mentors I met as a young adult was Carolyn Webb de Macias. At the time she was the Vice President of External Affairs for the University of Southern California and truly a force to be reckoned with. Her career spanned from corporate to local government to higher education. She was breaking the glass ceiling at every corner, yet she moved with grace, strength, confidence, and extreme humility. We met through the Los Angeles African American Women's Policy Institute and she was a board member and shared her experience of navigating corporate America, the community, and politics. We were encouraged during that first session of the 4-month program to reach out to the board members and seek out a mentor.

Well, I was no fool. I knew who I was going to ask. I called Carolyn the following week and asked if she would mentor me. She graciously accepted, responding jokingly, "Sure, but is there a class I need to take to mentor you?"

The relationship has blossomed over the last nine plus years - it will be 10 years of awakenings in January 2015. She has been a constant voice of reason when I feel the need to move with haste, but also challenges me to capture opportunities when they are around.

She has played a significant role in my career, initially bringing me to Los Angeles City Hall as a policy analyst in the Mayor's administration in 2005 and most recently encouraging me to apply to the White House Fellowship program within 48 hours of the deadline. While selected as a regional finalist, I didn't receive the fellowship; however, I was invited to interview with federal agencies and was selected to join the team at the U.S. Department of Health and Human Services implementing health information technology throughout the country. Who knew that her "gentle" nudge would open so many doors from impacting a community to a nation?

Mentors have played a critical role in my development and awakening, understanding my potential often times better than myself. As evidenced in most of my mentors, I typically am attracted to humble personalities in mentors, individuals that do not seek public gratification for the work that they have done, but it is received naturally because of the impact that they have made on others. The mentors I've had, all have awakened a sense of awareness, gratitude, purpose and really a commitment to community and uplifting others.

They are there to push you and motivate you when you doubt yourself; they have been that inner voice that speaks to me and says,

"You can do this! We have a higher expectation of you. There's no reason that you can't just try." These individuals I trust to give me honest feedback and they do, some gentler than others, but I am appreciative either way. Through their own insight, they have seen beyond my potential, which is why they are able to provide the guidance for my career, personal life and really encourage me to take it to the next level, thinking bold and big.

As mentees we have a critical responsibility to return the favor and reach out to others that may be in need of guidance or an awakening. I don't limit myself to who I can mentor, but I do try to be conscious of the words and guidance that I do provide others in hopes that they find reward or contentment in the mentoring relationship, but also for them to realize that they have a responsibility to return the favor again and to mentor the next person. Mentoring is cyclical.

Barbara Perkins - The Coach

Barbara Perkins is one of the individuals that I have come to rely upon as a coach/mentor; she has been a constant thread throughout the last 10 years. Whether it is a new job I am entering or seeking balance with life's priorities, Barbara has always been a healthy soundboard for reflection for really thinking about being intentional and living with purpose. She has dedicated herself to mentoring the next generation so that they too may answer the call of giving back.

Taking time out of your schedule to check on your mentee as well as your mentor, because this is a two-way relationship, is a critical component to an active mentor relationship.

Let's keep awakening the potential in others through this beautiful act of mentoring. The world is waiting.

Brenda Darcel Harris-Lee
President/CEO, California Black Health Network
The Blessing of Mentoring - God's Very Personal Gift to Me

As I drove up to the small, modest home in a low-income section of Nashville, TN, I was a bit nervous and unsure about what to expect. I had recently joined Big Sisters of Nashville and this was my very first opportunity to serve as a mentor and a guide. I wondered if the young lady with whom I had been matched, would accept me. Would she be shy or retiring? Would she even talk to me? I just didn't know what to expect. As her mom, a single mother opened the door, she greeted me with a warm and welcoming smile, and standing behind her, taller and more "mature" than I had anticipated, was her daughter, Rhonda. Slowly, she stepped from behind her mom, and ever so gingerly she offered that same smile that her mom had flashed just a few seconds before. And that was the beginning.

I developed not only a relationship with Rhonda, but I became a mentor to Rhonda's younger brother, Michael, as well. I just could not stand the lonely, lost look in his eyes when I would arrive to pick-up Rhonda, so I took them both. The year was 1977 and I was blessed to work with those two young jewels for the next three years. Unfortunately, they moved away and I lost touch with them, but the experience of mentoring those two youngsters shaped my life in ways that still have an impact to this very day.

The Oxford School of Coaching and Mentoring defines mentoring as "a powerful personal development and empowerment tool. It is an effective way of helping people to progress in their careers and is becoming increasing popular as its potential is realized. It is a partnership between two people - mentor and mentee - normally working in a similar field or sharing similar experiences. It is a helpful relationship based upon mutual trust and respect."

While mentoring Rhonda and Michael was certainly steeped in this definition, as time went on it became even more. You see, I never had children of my own. I did not know then that these two young people and so many after them would fill my life with the joys and the experiences that would last a lifetime. They were joys and experiences that only children can bring. But I also learned that it was my responsibility, my given destiny, to give back to the children that God had given to me – His guidance and His direction. Our children so desperately need for us to be an example; they need for us to be their role models and their guides. In later years and to this day I have found mentoring to be a basic tenant of both my professional and personal life. Mentoring anchors me. It reminds me of my purpose and my plan. The ability to share these gifts that God has shared with me; to pass on the knowledge and wisdom of my elders and my ancestors; to have some small stake in preparing the next generation for greatness… all of this defines the "why" in the work that I do each and every day.

In the mid 1980's I travelled to South Africa with a group of twelve other meeting-planning professionals. At the time, I owned a meeting-planning company and we were blessed to have been invited by the South African government to visit their country in an effort to assure us that South Africa had changed and now welcomed African American tourists and travelers. Of course, they wanted us to bring our business to South Africa to boost their economy and increase their tourism revenue. Assigned to our group was a young African female guide with whom I became enchanted. She spoke perfect English and had an engaging and ever-so kind demeanor. During the week that we spent in Johannesburg, Durbin and Soweto, I was privileged to get to know her well and soon we were both convinced that our meeting should become a long-term relationship.

I took Maklia on as a mentee. For years, we corresponded, exchanging letters and phone calls. I was able to watch from a distance as Maklia grew, matured, and completed her education. The successes she achieved made my heart sing, and the heartaches she experienced were as devastating to me as if she were my own birth daughter. But through it all, the experience of giving and taking, listening for understanding, and mentoring her in a non-judgmental circle of unconditional love and carefully directed guidance, not only served to help Maklia achieve her goals and change her life, but also allowed me to grow and prosper in ways that I had not expected or anticipated.

You see, mentoring is as much for the mentor as it is for the mentee. Through this wonderful art of sharing, I have learned to be transparent. I have learned to trust and to be open and honest, even when it's hard to do so. I have grown to know the value of allowing a person to come inside my soul, take a seat and peel away the layers of carefully constructed protection that can get in the way of genuine learning, deep revelation, and unfettered guidance. Mentoring has taught me the beauty of unconditional love and the grace of immediate and complete forgiveness. Mentoring has contributed to allowing me to bask in the growth and development of a number of young people who are now whole, successful and accomplished adults.

As President and CEO of California Black Health Network (CBHN), I have the opportunity to run a statewide non-profit that provides leadership around healthcare policy and advocacy. Often I attend meetings, conferences, conventions and events where I am the only African American voice in the room. I have made it a policy and a strategy to bring interns into our workplace. I want these young students to be the recipients of the knowledge and expertise that my diverse and experienced staff can provide. I want them to understand that if you are not at the table, you are probably on the menu.

At CBHN, we mentor and teach our young people, allowing them to attend events and meetings, even legislative hearings that they might not ordinarily get to observe. We guide them, we nurture our young men and women and we provide for them a safe haven for making the mistakes they are bound to make, and then, with care and guidance, allowing them to grow and develop by correcting their course and moving on, moving forward.

It is my hope, my prayer, that the mentoring I have been privileged to provide and the young people whose lives I have been blessed to touch will ultimately become my legacy. For it is said, "Keep putting into practice all you learned from me and heard from me and saw me doing, and the God of peace will be with you." Philippians 4:9 (New English Translation)

Cody W. Perkins
Student and Photographer
Mentorship of My Life

Every young person can benefit from having a mentor. I believe that it is important that young people have someone in their life to guide them and show them by example of how to get multiple aspects of their lives on track whether it is professional, educational, or emotional. My upbringing was different. By the grace of God, I was born into a family of givers that showed me by example that even when times are tough, you can still be reliable and helpful to those in need around you. I didn't have a solid mentor, but I was lucky enough to be surrounded by all sorts of people, good and bad, who taught how to gain useful knowledge from everyone that I was around. Whether it is a highly respected city official to the neighborhood alcoholic, my parents did not shelter me from the realities of the world growing up. I can definitely say that I am a product of the environment that my parents had built for me. With both of them being busy professionals, I had people looking after me very protectively. I had nannies from South America, my grandmother from the south, and my godmother from the east coast. I had babysitters that were very religious and babysitters that were young.

I benefited the most because, at a young age, I was able to know and respect people of all nationalities and backgrounds. I learned to respect people regardless of who they were. These were the foundations of my becoming the "people person" that I am today.

As I got older and more independent, I fell in love with the arts and was involved in a lot of extracurricular activities that really shaped the person I am today. With the help of some great artists who found it important to teach kids, mentor them and show them the ropes of the industry, including perfecting your craft to networking and learning how to work a room with other professionals. Eartha Robinson and Vernee Watson, aside from my mother and my godmother, were two women who really took me under their wings. They showed me the ropes and made sure I was prepared socially to handle myself in the cutthroat world of entertainment. Their teachings spilled over into me being prepared for anything life would bring to me. Being a part of the performance art community of young talented kids with these amazing adults to show us the way, while they are still committed to their careers, was a big shift for me. I was being influenced to apply all of this information to my life. These talented ladies unselfishly led our performance group of 12-people strong. We are all like brothers and sisters and they are still like our mothers, even today at 25 years old.

Now that I have completed my schooling and I am striving to jump-start my career, I really could use a mentor in my field. I need someone to guide me in the right direction, assist me to set goals, evaluate my efforts to complete those goals, and to groom me to strengthen my self-confidence. The fashion entertainment industry is such a closed-off industry, but I have learned that once you are in, you are in!

I have worked in New York City and had two internships. But, there is nothing like having that one-on-one connection with someone who can vouch for you and inform you of the dos and don'ts of the industry. I am currently self-mentoring, self-empowering and slowly absorbing. I am making sure that every step I take is planned out. I recognize I could use some nurturing assistance, other than my parents, who are not involved in this particular industry I want to be in. I am so accustomed to having people all around me, guiding me, but as an adult, the primary people I have access to are my peers and colleagues. Unfortunately, they are not necessarily on the same track that I would like to follow.

I also find myself wanting to work with children now that I am older. I believe that I could be a positive influence because of my blessings while some of these kids have not received much guidance or feel misunderstood or awkward. I can understand that because during my childhood I often felt out of place. Sometimes people need reassurance or for someone to let them know they are on the right path and doing things correctly or incorrectly.

Mentoring is important to shaping the perspective of our youth and their future. It is extremely necessary. If I did not have the people in my life that have guided me, I don't know what path I would have taken. I see some of the people I grew up with who had no role models and were not provided with guidance are now completely broke, have to start over in their mid-twenties, and are lost because they have no idea what they want to do with their lives, or what they can contribute to the world. I am thankful to all my mentors for showing me the ropes, and making me feel so solid and confident in the world today.

Janeen Uzzell
Executive, General Electric
LET YOUR UNIQUENESS BE CENTER STAGE

Originally I am from Newark, NJ. My dad came up from the South, worked hard to take care of his family and later moved us to Plainfield, NJ. I had a chance to go to a boarding school called Mt. Saint Mary's Academy in Watchung, NJ. I consider my sister a mentor in that she was twelve years older than I and had a major influence on convincing my parents to let me go to that school. I worked hard and got into Lehigh University, an Ivy League school in Pennsylvania on an engineering scholarship that ran out sooner than my education. Luckily, I was an active member of the National Society of Black Engineers (NSBE), which later afforded me an opportunity that I certainly was not aware of at the time.

While I was attending a NSBE conference, one of our advisors named Dr. Sharp from North Carolina A&T, the Dean of Mechanical Engineering, told me that if I needed to transfer schools he would give me a scholarship to A&T. Needless to say, I transferred to where I had free money and no debt. After I graduated, I went back to New Jersey for work and then I moved to Washington, D.C. where I started my global role. I had assignments in Indonesia, Bangladesh, and Africa. In terms of becoming a global leader, taking on those international duties is what became the game changer for me.

As a Black woman, from the position of having a mentor in my life, I particularly feel like mentorship gave me benchmarks and levels to aspire to. Even as an adult executive, I still position myself in the eyes of others I admire, that challenge me to dream bigger and push harder. I think it's critical because we are surrounded by negative influences and the opportunity to have someone actually commit to encouraging your career is special.

Two people who had major influence on my life were a white male and a black woman. Glen MacAuthor, the white male, was the person who focused on pivoting my career and transitioned my career from being a great *engineer* to being what he saw in me as becoming a great *leader*. He was the one who told me I had potential beyond engineering and that I could choose to sit in the dungeon and code all day or use the talents he saw in me to go beyond. Glen is the reason I left the telecommunications industry and went to General Electric (GE) to develop my leadership qualities. As a woman in engineering, I thought I had made it and was in a comfortable position from where I was sitting. I remember listening to my elder cousin tell me, "You're smart, you're good at math and science, and you should study engineering because you'll always have a job. Plus, there are not a lot of women who do it so you should go for it." Although that was true, I no longer wanted to settle for being just a female engineer.

The woman that mentors me still to this day is Paula Madison. She was an officer at the GE Corporation who led businesses at NBC Universal and even now continues to do amazing things. Being a graduate student, I was considering GE as a company that I wanted to look into for work. I remember specifically sitting under the dryer at my hairdresser, about fourteen years ago, talking to the girl next to me and I leaned over to show her the article I was reading. There was a Black woman sitting behind a huge desk. It was a GE ad; her image had such power and strength. At the time I did not know who she was nor the impact would she have on my life. I just knew I wanted to meet her and get something from her. The woman's name was Paula Madison who happens to be the woman who, 13 years later, is now my mentor and good friend.

True story: A year and a half later, I was hired by GE and attended their African American symposium. It was my first year in the company and I remember seeing the woman from the magazine on the panel. I went up to her to ask for time on her calendar and I recall her saying to me, "People come to events like this and everyone gets inspired, but only a third of the people actually follow up with me. So we will see if you actually call." I tried for months to get on her calendar. I think she wanted to see how serious I was.

For years I met with Paula to explain my metrics and go over my career goals in the company. After she saw that I knew what I was doing, the conversation began to change and shift more towards areas that pushed and annoyed me, like dating, what I wanted out of life, and what were my personal goals. Then there was a period when I experienced a lot of loss and had to take care of my family. Fortunately for me, Paula helped me to keep my sanity, and be okay with turning down promotions in order to take care of myself. Other people in the company knew she was my mentor, and I always respected her for putting her neck on the line when referring me for things. I think about my mentors like I consider my family when I have to make decisions. Having Paula as my mentor is monumental. She is rock solid and when she talks people listen. Paula made my career navigation strategies make sense.

From a leadership perspective, the lesson I gathered from Paula is to know your space well, gain access, help develop others to make your circles even bigger, and remember that mentoring is not a one-way street and that mentors are also learning from mentees.

Although I am back in the states, for many years I have been living in West Africa conducting business for GE. I was a part of building out their business footprint in the Healthcare space. I was based in Ghana, but I covered all of the sub-Saharan Africa. It was both a life and career changing experience. It led me to my next promotion. I became a Senior Executive in the company, and it did major things for my career and personal life. I know that Paula was very influential in picking me to go.

I noticed that when my role in leadership began changing, my relationships shifted and I had to own that by embracing my own maturity, acknowledge when it was time to let things go and evolve into the next phase. During those transitions I noticed that I stood a chance of being a mentor, a coach or in a position where I made myself accessible to others without judgment. I personally believe that as people of color, we all must be accountable for the positions we seek.

It's interesting because I feel that mentoring relationships change positions where you can become peers and start sharing things as opposed to seeking advice. When you show up in the world, be clear about what you have to offer.

Mentoring is trusted advisory and something you ask for that is very relational. It transcends long-term and has more depth, whereas coaching can be situational yet equally as important as mentoring. For example, Paula is my mentor but she has also coached me in certain areas of my life as well. Another person that has been a mentor and a coach is Barbara Perkins. I met Barbara through Paula Madison. There is something in Barbara that I can't exactly pinpoint right now, but it is something special and I believe there is some advice and guidance that she will provide in the future.

In my current position at General Electric, I do two things that I really love. I manage a technology business development team at the research center where I lead a team of scientists and engineers in business development, a mixture of business and technology. Who would have thought that I could make a huge career out of Science, Technology, Engineering and Math (STEM) education that would become so huge that it's on top of the minds of our President and leaders around the world?

First and foremost, I am an ordinary girl that has taken advantage of the things that I have been exposed to as well as the doors that have been closed in front of me. It is important to know that nothing that I am doing is out of your reach! So, be bold, have grit, do not be afraid, and know that no matter what anybody says, you are enough!

Meshelle
Comedienne/Award Winning Playwright/Author
ORGANIC MENTORING

At the onset, I cannot explain, but the first word that my fingers typed when I thought of this gracious endeavor was meaning. I'm assuming that my selective and genetic subconscious knows something that my consciousness will catch up to in a few stanzas. Essentially, there is meaning semantically and etymologically to the word mentor[ing]. According to Webster's online Dictionary http://www.merriam-webster.com/dictionary/mentor, mentor is a verb, which means: to teach or give advice or guidance to (someone, such as a less experienced person or a child). The more I attempted to make sense or meaning of mentoring, my curiosity grew, wanting to consider its origin/etymology. It is largely of Greek origin (mentor (n.) "wise advisor," 1750, from Greek Mentor, perhaps ultimately meaning "adviser," because the name appears to be an agent noun of mentos "intent, purpose, spirit, passion"). Further, in Sanskrit it derives from (man-tar "one who thinks") and in Latin (mon-i-tor "one who admonishes"). My scholarly itch was scratched leaving the heart of the matter up for grand consideration.

I have been blessed to be mentor and mentee in a little over 4 short decades of living, and if my exchanges thus far are any indication of what lies ahead, I am giddy with expectation and undaunted by the challenge that these opportunities will present. As an inner-city girl born to a teen mother who was the oldest of nine children born to her young southern parents, I benefited firsthand from my teen mother's zeal for council and guidance wrapped in an educable spirit.

My maternal grandparents where teen newlyweds and the offspring of lay farmers, share croppers and skilled laborers, whose quest to live a better life led them to head north. Neither of them graduated from high school. My grandmother was just one year shy of graduation when she learned of her first pregnancy, while my grandfather never completed elementary school, and was unable to read or write. He married my grandmother and used his sharp wit and god-given ability to repair nearly anything mechanical to care for his wife and children.   Frankly, outside of a fierce love for God, cleanliness, family solidarity, insistence on "good manners" and relentless work ethic (which were rich nonetheless), my grandparents didn't have much to offer their oldest daughter when she yearned for insight in navigating her professional and academic life post-pregnancy.

My mother, a sweet hardworking teen, completed her general requirements and proved to be a proficient typist, communicator and naturally navigated to women who seemed to have skill sets that she admired and she thought would advance their personal and professional lives. Organically, they'd invite her to gatherings in their personal and professional circles and she would bring my sister and me along, affording us the accouterments of their lives. This was our life. My mom read articles they suggested, subscribed to magazines and attended free classes and lectures at their advisement. While they varied in age, ideology, skill set and ethnicity, these women in particular, changed the fabric of my mom's life and ostensibly shifted our paradigm for the rest of our lives.   It was never defined as "mentoring" at the time, although that was exactly the case.

My mother's world, dreams, aspirations and expectations grew immensely beyond the offerings of her immediate culture and environment. As a result, a teen, a high school dropout single mother, renting apartments, became a married college graduate, with impeccable credit and homeowner, and those are just the tags that give levity to this analogy. The legacy of mentoring she cultivated has led both my sister and I to not only mentor, but seek mentee opportunities.

The reciprocity that is the essence of mentoring is infinite; rendering it impossible to feel alone in navigating next steps in any area of my life. I give what I have seen and received, therefore, mentoring is as organic as inhaling and exhaling, without it, my existence would be null and void. It's instructed and informed to make myself available organically (a chance meeting) and systemically (as Founder/Executive Director, of Goal-diggers The Sankofa Project www.meshelle.net/goaldiggers) to the same population that is oftentimes counted out, much like my mom was so many years ago. My heart's work is steeped in serving/mentoring underserved urban and rural girls, aiding them in their quest for the highest level of education, while unearthing their ethnic identity to ensure a positive self-concept. They must be armed to tell their stories with unapologetic clarity and truth. One of my templates for that example is the book I penned and curriculum, "101 Things Every Girl/Young Woman of Color Should Know" (Duafe Press, 2010) and "The Power of Knowing: 101 Things Every Girl/Young Woman of Color Should Know THE WORKBOOK". My hope is that while we have an undeniable, palpable exchange, there must be materials that aid, speaks to and further the lives of one another. These are my intentions; therefore, organic mentoring leaves those involved compelled to favorably tip the karmic scales!

I PRESS...
MESHELLE "The Indie-Mom of Comedy"

Juwana Todd
Day Spa & Salon Owner
Friendship And Mentoring

As a young woman ready to conquer the world, I opened my own small beauty salon. Barbara Perkins was a faithful client who, in her own way, would challenge me to be better. She would hold me accountable to be professional. She has been a part of my life for over 17 years. I had a lot of clients, but she was different. There has always been something about her that was intriguing.

After several years of servicing Barbara and getting to know her, we built a trust and friendship. I remember that she invited me to her house for dinner. I must say, her home was fabulous. Meeting with her was so eye opening. She gave me an interest in politics, which is my major now. She sparked my interest in community needs. I realized, after meeting with her, that my responsibility was greater than I had imagined. Mentoring is not always formal. The exposure that I have experienced in Ms. Barbara's presence was always impressive. I've met doctors, lawyers, politicians and one of my personal aspirations, Iyanla Vanzant.

One of my favorite events with Ms. Barbara was, a Sisters at the Well event, with about 30 women of all ages. We met at City Walk for coffee and to catch a limo to caravan all of us to the outlets to do some shopping. But of course, she had something up her sleeve that was so powerful. Barbara told the story of how she came up with the concept of Sisters at the Well, and how that was the place of gathering for conversation and sisterhood. She had all of us pull a rock with a word on it from a basket.

It was an exercise for us to share what that word meant in our lives. Everyone began to share and it was so powerful because emotions were high. People who looked so well put-together had amazing testimonies of struggles, valleys and endurance. It affected me, bringing out emotions that had not been realized. It was so powerful and cleansing. After shopping, we proceeded to her home in Palm Springs for dinner to listen to poetry and women connecting. It was great.

I've had the opportunity to work with Ms. Barbara on her, We See You Award Show, to provide the hair and the makeup for the honorees. Being the "Glam Squad" is a pleasure, but the real pleasure is meeting women that have done some amazing work.

Every time I leave an event or session with Ms. Barbara, I leave feeling like I have so much work to do. She inspires me. She motivates me beyond what I can see. I am a woman of faith and I know that God has placed her in my life for guidance and support. She's mentored me in business decisions, through divorce and as a parent. I am truly grateful to have Ms. Barbara in my life.

Tiffany Ferguson
Entrepreneur
Paying it Forward

As I think back to my childhood growing up in a church, the women showed us overwhelming love and provided a sense of comfort and safety. Mentoring showed up differently in my life from as early as I can remember. It started in church. The older women in the church, who we all referred to as "the church mothers," would sing songs of praise over the children and literally pray for you in front of the church attendees during service. They appointed themselves responsible for the children having learned manners and proper church etiquette.

As a young woman when I became a mother, there were others who came into my life to help guide me and provide another level of wisdom and maturity for me. Mentoring took on a more important meaning for me. Not only was I to benefit from having mentors, I also learned how to become a mentor to my son and to other young people around me. My siblings now look to me for the same guidance that I had looked to others for. Of those whom I have mentored, a requirement is that they be the best that they can be.

I believe that God uses even children to help other children. Peer to peer mentoring can be more impactful than adult to child mentoring. Children are influenced by their peers positively and unfortunately too often negatively. Everyone who comes into your life with advice is not necessarily a mentor. I am a woman of tremendous faith and I try to live my life as a God-loving, God-fearing woman. I consider it a blessing to be able to help shape someone else's life and this blessing I do not take for granted.

When I have been asked to mentor someone, I would first question their needs, their goals and get to understand their needs. I would also share with them that my mentoring is influenced by my level of expertise, experiences, knowledge and spiritual beliefs. Mentoring requires some level of like-mindedness. There are expectations placed on both the mentor and mentee in these relationships. I believe it is best that expectations are discussed in advance.

Open and good communication is very important and a necessity with mentoring. As passionate as I am about the power of mentoring, I am also very passionate about the fact that too many children are without guidance or role models and without the assistance they need to develop successfully. Mentoring is free. It only costs time to assist someone. I have committed myself to providing a helping hand and sharing my mentoring skills.

I am also thankful to many women in my life that have helped me along the way. Barbara Perkins is one of them. I've known her for over a decade and have serviced her as a natural hair stylist. She sits in my chair and shares wisdom freely and often. She provides me with inspiration and motivation and for this I am truly grateful.

Lula Bailey Ballton, Ph.D.
President, Lula Ballton & Associates, Inc.

My Mentor: Mrs. Ollie Allen

When I first sat down on her back porch, I was 9 years old, and barefoot. I just stared at a humming bird as it flew down to her honeysuckle-covered fence. I did not want to talk to anyone about the chaos that was happening at my middle-class home. I did not want one more person to tell me how fortunate we were to have so much...stuff.

I lived in a small town and went to a tiny Presbyterian church. Mrs. Allen was the Pastor's wife. She had no biological children. However, she mentored and nurtured the dozen of us who came through the church "Youth Fellowship." In the midst of all her "church kids" she took me (I thought I was the only one) under her wings. She helped me see and experience beyond the small world I lived in, beyond the bland midwestern town and my home life drama.

On her porch she talked to me about places I could visit like Axum, Ethiopia, where the "Ark of the Covenant" was reported to be, or Atlanta, Georgia, where there were 5 Black colleges.

Mrs. Allen talked about the people I could and should meet. She shared with me books that we could read together. I walked to her house many days. In the spring and summers, I sat on her porch steps, watched birds and bugs move through and around her garden. When the weather was cool, I sat at her kitchen table watching her move about, making food and crafts. Sometimes I joined her in her tasks. No matter where or what the activity, I was feeling my feelings and listening to her words, which usually drained my angst. When I headed to my house, my mind was filled with new thoughts and the world's possibilities. It was like a soothing warm blanket of words and ideas.

Whenever I came to her house, I always left with something. Sometimes she gave me a poem, like Langston Hughes' "Mother to

Son…" or "Life for me ain't been no crystal stair…" or a quotation like Eleanor Roosevelt's, "No one can make you feel inferior without your permission." Sometimes I even left with a song and always a HUG.

Once she introduced me to James Weldon's book, GOD'S TROMBONES. At school they told us about one poem in the book, "The Creation." Mrs. Allen shared the other dozen or so poems in the book with me. I subsequently won many oratorical contests with the poem "The Judgment Day" from it. In fact, it led me, like it did Oprah Winfrey, to a Speech Scholarship in college.

She introduced me to writers, Gene Toomer and Langston Hughes - people I had never heard of at the white schools I attended. Because of Mrs. Allen, I found "me" in literature and performance and began to see there was value in "My Story."

Every Tuesday and Friday her dozen church kids met in our church basement. We ate, played games, practiced our songs for the youth choir and went home. None of us knew that more than that was happening to and with us.

She read to us while we ate. Through and above our protests, she introduced us to new foods: oysters, bruschetta, eggplant, mushrooms and much more!

We sang songs from various cultures and in various languages. One of us became a concert violinist because of her exposure. From our little town, with so few Black people, he went on to be a classical tenor, violinist and a music professor at the University of Michigan.

At 14, I was still walking to her house, sitting on the back steps, staring out into her yard, getting spiritual direction, emotional support and plain old good advice. She made me memorize scriptures so I "would be equipped and armed" when I needed "spiritual weapons."

When my mind got clouded she gave me Philippians 4:8, "Think on these things…" When I was afraid, Psalm 23. At 30, I got robbed at gunpoint in my home. The perpetrator kept asking questions and I could only respond in the Scripture, "The Lord is my Shepherd… Though I walk through the shadow of death I will fear no evil…" He finally got frustrated, took his gun and left my home. Thank you, Mrs. Allen.

When I was 16, my home life got more dramatic. During my family explosions, I started walking to her house and she'd invite me to talk about it. She still fed me exotic food, played classical music and had me read to her from the classics. She invited me to write. Write my story and write down my feelings. She would correct my writing to improve my skill, but never my story.

From 16-18 she took us, her church kids, to see a Broadway play, to hear Marian Anderson in concert. She even introduced me to Jessye Norman, the famous Black Contralto who was only 2 years older than me.

As my personal mentor, she helped me create a platform upon which I could stand and grow. She gave me a mirror that reflected that this little Black girl see more than her meager surrounding reflected. My worldview expanded, even exploded!

Over the years, we spent many hours on her back steps, at her kitchen table as well as in the church fellowship hall. I had no idea I was being mentored, until I was 41 and Mrs. Allen died. My mother included in Mrs. Allen's obituary that, while she and all the mothers were in their 20's and 30's, growing up and maturing in love and life, "Mrs. Ollie Allen nurtured and raised our children. She loved them and provided them a success path. To her we will be eternally grateful."

Only then did I understand what a real mentor is and does. Thank you, Mrs. Allen.

Danny J. Bakewell, Jr.
Executive Editor, The Los Angeles Sentinel
IT TAKES A VILLAGE

Mentorship plays a vital role in the success and development of people in general. Whether you are young or old, everyone needs mentorship. Each of us has an inherent responsibility to give back to those who follow us and pass down from one generation to the next the knowledge, wisdom and understanding that one gains through life's experiences. Whether your experiences in life are good or bad, the benefits of that knowledge passed on to those who follow you will have and will always be the cornerstone for people and a community's growth and prosperity.

Mentorship is even more vital within the African American community. As the image of African Americans within the main stream media diminishes and as society continues to promote, profit and propagandize the worst of Black life, it is only through the actual experiences and interaction of mentors that can show our young people that success is not in the collection of material things, but in the legacy of empowerment that we leave and give to the next generation that follows.

I have been blessed to have some great mentors in my life. My parents Danny and Aline Bakewell, Sr. have been the most influential mentors (role models) in my life. While they are extremely different in the way they pass on their knowledge, they have both played a key role in my development as a man, as a parent, as a businessman, and as a servant to my community.

My parents should and always will be my first line of mentors, but Brenda Marsh-Mitchell, Curtis Owens, Coach Lalo Mendoza and my fraternity brother, Billy DeBerry (Kappa Alpha Psi), are also major mentors in my personal and professional development. They assumed these roles without ever signing up for the job, none of them volunteered to mentor me, but their influence, guidance and commitment to me and my well-being will forever be appreciated.

I have learned so much from the mentors in my life, and the knowledge, guidance and experiences that they passed on to me. Their willingness to openly share and to pull my coat and kick my ass when necessary, have enhanced my own willingness and ability to mentor those who follow me.

We must understand our roles as mentors, we must be willing to put forth the effort and do so without personal glory, but understand and receive the satisfaction of seeing someone else prosper with knowledge that our input, in some large or small way, has played a part in their success.

I believe more than anything else that I was put on this earth and blessed by God to be a coach. If I could go back and do it all over again I would have made the decision to be a football coach. I have received time and time again a satisfaction from coaching that I have not received from any other endeavor I have ever undertaken. But somewhere a long time ago I made the decision to go in another direction, and that is okay. I now use the skills that I developed on the football field to help mentor and develop the staff at the Los Angeles Sentinel, the staff at The Bakewell Company, the team who works on putting on The Taste of Soul, the largest outdoor community festival in Los Angeles, and I use these skills to help develop young men and women in everything I undertake.

I never do these things looking for personal glory or accolades; I do these things because the tasks I undertake, I believe, make for a better life for the people in my community, for the people in my family, and my friends. I reap great rewards from seeing a job well done.

I am not one who believes that only men can mentor men; however, in today's climate, I do believe that only a man can teach a man how to me a man. African American men in particular need other African American men to teach them how to navigate the often-troubled waters of our society. Some things can only be taught from the actual experiences and challenges that an African American male has gone through for it to be fully grasped.

It is like trying to explain colors to a person who has been blind their entire life, or trying to explain the experience of childbirth to a man. We can empathize with the experience, but we can never truly understand the process. "Only a Black man understands the twisted feeling you get in the pit of your stomach when you see the flashing red lights behind you from the police. The sense of vulnerability, it doesn't matter how old you are or how successful you are, how guilty or innocent you may be; you are completely overwhelmed by a sense of hopelessness. Your survival mode kicks in and, unfortunately, that sense and need for survival is the very thing that gets too many of our Black men killed."

In my lifetime I have had the privilege of learning from some of the greatest leaders in our community, Dr. Thomas Kilgore, Bishop H. H. Brookins, Pastor H. H. Lusk, the Reverend Cecil "Chip" Murray, Walter Bremond, Lillian Mobley, Mary Henry and Johnnie Tillman. Each of these people interjected into me a sense of responsibility and a dedication to my community.

This year I lost one of my greatest mentors in Brenda Marsh-Mitchell. This woman was not only a mentor to me, my other mother, but she was my friend. She taught me the importance of faith, in giving everything to God, and instilled in me a work ethic that has and will last my entire life. She probably never knew she was mentoring me and I certainly did not realize that I was her mentee, but the truth is she was my mentor and I was her mentee. I learned from her the importance of doing the right thing even when no one was looking. Her loss has affected me more than I would have ever imagined, probably because I never imagined life without her. That is the true gift of mentorship, the ability to influence life directly or indirectly in a positive way without ever seeking glory or recognition for oneself, but rejoicing in knowing, "JOB WELL DONE!"

The Magic of MENTORING
PEARLS of WISDOM

What Now?

I began this book with a special acknowledgement of Dr. Myles Monroe, a man of humble beginnings, whose life and work demonstrated what he believed was his charge and his God-given responsibility while here on this earth. I believe as he did: we each have special orders given to us by our Creator. I further believe that far too many people die without being complete. Far too many people leave this earth not realizing that there was more for them to do and to be. They miss out on the joys of completion.

When Dr. Myles Monroe, his wife, and six other members of his church family all died in an accidental plane crash on November 9, 2014, it seemed like all the people on the islands of the Bahamas held their breath at the learning of this tragic news. Then as the news spread across the world, millions of people took to social media, expressing their sadness in postings and millions more expressing the joy they had in knowing Dr. Monroe or having heard him speak or the joy they received in reading one of his books. What I did not read in the many posts and expressions were regrets about his dying.

The people knew by the life and work of Dr. Monroe that he was on a mission. He was on his mission to complete what he believed was his assignment. He would often say that he wanted to complete his mission and make room for the new leadership that would emerge once he was gone. He would say that he wanted to cheat the grave by doing all of his work while alive. No one knows the time or the circumstances by which the journey of this life will be over. Even those who are diagnosed with terminal illnesses do not really know when they will take their last breath on this earth.

My beloved mother, Barbara Parrish, died on January 17, 2011. Seven months prior to her death, while she was lying in the hospital in Fort Lauderdale, Florida, connected to a ventilator, not breathing on her own, I received a call from my dear sister Debra, telling me that the doctors had just informed her that our mother had about 24 to 48 hours to live. Speaking from what they knew about the science of medicine and speaking from their years of experiences, they concluded that we as a family should make the decision to remove our mother from all of the life sustaining machinery that the exact same medical team had placed her on.

My request to speak with the primary physician resulted in the same conclusions and forceful recommendation to pull the plug on our mother. As I sat in my living room in Sylmar, California, contemplating the five and a half hours flight to Florida, mother's home since moving from California where she lived with and near to me for fourteen years, I began to hear the soothing whispers from deep within me. These lyrics came to my mind.

Little Girls
by Patti Labelle

Little girls
Sleep at night
Safe inside their dreams, is it a scheme
They think they'll grow up, into girls
I am old, I am young and wise
I'm just a little girl that came close
Who hides behind a face
But really knows

If you devise what a child get for free
And I'll be viewed that way once of me

Come on and hold me tight
Don't turn off the light
Just let your words embrace me
Like a father's loving arms
Protect me from the night - it will be alright
'Cause tonight I'm just a little girl

This song gave me peace for the moment and reminded me that life is so very fragile. It took me back to the little girl who wanted to make my mother proud someday. I could think back on how many things I did to get her attention and how important it is for every little girl and boy to have someone they want to make proud and who inspires them to be the best they can be.

Mentoring is the biggest and most important gift we can give to a child. Mentoring works, we need to fully understand its value and set a clear intention for each relationship. Certainly, it begins as early as possible and can be a life-long, life-enhancing process. There are women of diverse ages in my life that I mentor and just as important, there are women of diverse ages in my life who mentor me.

A mentoring relationship that has been nurtured and allowed to grow into a mutually beneficial engagement can be the most important relationship in one's life. It's in these types of relationships where there is equal balance in the commitment, equal balance in expectations, and equal balance in the many benefits that can be found. The critical question is, "Who are you mentoring?"

The 47 contributors to this book have shared their stories with passion and transparency. They are advocates for having more mentors nationally and abroad. Every child, regardless of their circumstances, deserves to be mentored. Organizations such as Mentoring USA, The National CARES Mentoring Movement, and President's Obama's new national initiative, My Brother's Keepers, are examples of the good work being done. However, if we are to reach all of our children, especially those youth that continue to be underserved and find themselves at significant risk for the far too many ailments that plague communities across America, we are going to have to do this one to one. Each of us must reach at least one. Each of us would need to represent that pearl in someone else's life.

An important question to ask yourself is, "What can I give to a young person?" "What would I want for my own children?" and "How can I be a positive influence in someone else's life?" Signing up to be a mentor does not mean you are signing up to be a parent, but you are expected to be a responsible adult or a level-headed peer. Mentoring is mostly about listening and being. Being present fulfills half the need. Young people want to know that they matter. They want to know that someone truly cares about them, and they want to safely dream their dreams with positive reinforcement and gentle guidance when needed.

Therefore, my question to you is what now? What will you do now? Who are you mentoring? If you are mentoring, is the relationship working? How would your mentee describe the relationship that you have? How do you assess the relationship, and what are the mutual expectations?

Sometimes it can be difficult to know if the mentoring relationship is working for both you and the mentee. It is important to ensure that the communication flow is good. Another proven way to determine if you are getting the maximum benefit from your mentoring relationship is to spend time with other mentors and mentees. The group-mentoring model has tremendous benefits that can help to improve your one-to-one mentoring. It's not okay to just wish and hope that you are making a difference in the life of your mentee. There are tools, training, and many books that can help you. I urge you to do the work necessary to give both you and your mentee the added advantage of getting the maximum from the relationship.

The need for mentors in this country is at an all-time high. The need for black mentors is even higher. The need for black male mentors is at the crisis-level in the nation. Black men are the last group to step up when asked to make this commitment. Yet our black boys are desperate to find responsible men to be in their lives for the long haul. We can turn these statistics around if we ourselves identify men who have something special to offer a youngster. Give these men, your friends, family members, or peers encouragement to mentor.

In the six years that I spent working directly in the mentoring movement, I was privileged to speak with black men on a regular basis about mentoring. They would express their uncertainty about how to mentor or what is expected of them in a mentoring relationship. The lack of desire to mentor was rarely the case, but I would not have known that had I not been willing to have those conversations. My sense of the crisis and tremendous need for mentors is not that we don't have folks who *can*, but we have folks who don't *believe* they can. We can change that belief if we all become recruiters for mentors for our children.

Don't forget to have fun! The joy I get when hanging around the young women I mentor is priceless. When I began this book project, I did not know how many women I shared a mentor/mentee relationship with. Ten years ago, while serving as a faculty trainer for women interested in public policy, through a program I helped to launch with six other women leaders in Los Angeles, The Los Angeles African American Women Public Policy Institute, I decided that each year I would connect deeper with one of the twenty women after their graduation from the program. These relationships grew into very special and fun relationships. These women keep me smiling and current. They especially help me in the social media space and with fashion! It was a big surprise to me when I listed the names to find that ten of the seventeen women that I have mentored are from the LAAAWPPI program. They are all smart, beautiful inside and out, and they are just a joy in my life.

Conclusion

The call has been made! The solution is simple! The time is now! Would you be willing to do something today to advance the mission? Would you be willing to write in a journal what actions you will take this month? Would you be willing to let me know what you are doing differently? It would be great to know how this collection of stories has influenced others.

I shared with the 47 contributors to this book that this is our project. In the face of so many challenges that need our attention in communities across this country, it is tempting at times to feel that our ability to impact positive change is slim to none. I propose that together we can turn the catastrophic tide that seems to be heading directly toward us as black people in this country. This can be done if we would sign on to be the mapmakers for ourselves. These are not the worse times in the black experience. We can, if we believe we can. Let us change our communities, one person at a time, one household at a time, one block at a time, one neighborhood at a time, one city at a time, and one state at a time and then the nation. This is the movement, this is the charge, and we each have a part to play.

Will you be that missing Tahitian Pearl in your community? Let's make this magic together!

Thank You

Corina Mena-Aikhionbare
Maxine Attong
Debra Robinson Baker
Danny Bakewell, Jr.
Lula Bailey Ballton, Ph.D.
Charlotte (Char) Bland
Cheryl Brownlee
Darrell Brown
Brent F. Burton
Jacqueline Castillo
Wendy Dean
Avis Jones DeWeever, Ph.D.
Tiffany Ferguson
Melrita Evans Fortson
Juanita Holcombe Hamilton
Kellie Hawkins
Cynthia Mitchell Heard
Sheila Fleming Hunter, Ph.D.
Tammilee Jules
Maleena Lawrence
Brenda Darcel Harris-Lee
Rev. Deborah Chinaza Lee
Vanessa Leon
Rustin Lewis, Ph.D.
Alva Adams - Mason
Penelope Jones - Mensah Mawuenyega, Esq.
Meshelle Shields
Linda Morgan
Bridget Marie Nelson

Barbara A. Perkins
Cody W. Perkins
Kimberly Peters
Valerie Polk
Stephen Powell
Theresa Price
Ebonee Rice
Willa Robinson
April Quiana Russell
Rhonda Sams
Elsie L. Scott, Ph.D.
Juanita Palacios-Sims
Aubrey Stone
Dawn Sutherland
Juwana Todd
Naomi Turner
Janeen Uzzell
Erica Walden